C000303535

LINCOLNSH
HEADLINES
ADRIAN GRAY

LINCOLNSHIRE HEADLINES

★

ADRIAN GRAY

COUNTRYSIDE BOOKS
NEWBURY, BERKSHIRE

First Published 1993
© Adrian Gray 1993

All rights reserved. No reproduction
permitted without the prior permission
of the publishers:

COUNTRYSIDE BOOKS
3 Catherine Road
Newbury, Berkshire

ISBN 1 85306 261 8

Cover Design by Mon Mohan

Produced through MRM Associates Ltd., Reading
Typeset by Paragon Typesetters, Queensferry, Clwyd
Printed in England

Contents

*For Les and Bernie Large, purveyors of
many a good dinner (and glass of wine as well)*

Foreword

★

Despite popular images of monotonous fenland and un-restricted combine harvesters, Lincolnshire is a county that is full of character and interest. It has a varied and subtle landscape that hides many secrets such as its delightful villages and homely country towns.

Yet Lincolnshire is also a county that is full of history. Some of that history is well known – it has given the nation a King and two Prime Ministers – but many of the most interesting stories from its past have been quietly forgotten.

In this book I have tried to revive some of the most fascinating stories from the last 200 years of life in Lincolnshire. One or two stories are well-known even today, but others reveal some of the earthy secrets that caused a stir in bygone days. What is given here can only be a sample, for the life of Lincolnshire teems with the stories of strange folk and peculiar events. Hopefully there are some here to suit every appetite.

Adrian Gray
Ruskington 1993

The Skegness Pleasure Boat Disaster

★

The town of Skegness enjoyed a meteoric rise to fame as a coastal resort during the later years of the 19th century. In 1871 its entire population had amounted to a mere 349 hardy souls, but the opening of the railway in 1873 changed this small community for ever. The 9th Earl of Scarborough began his scheme to build a new town and a pier was opened in 1881. The following summer the trains brought in 230,000 excursionists – an incredible number for a town that had hardly featured on a map only ten years before. New facilities, like the public baths, were added each year and the town seemed set for a period of limitless success until the shadow of tragedy was cast over it.

Saturday 8th July, 1893 seemed to be a normal summer day at Skegness – a town that was just entering its most glorious phase as a resort for holidaymakers. That morning, the railway station was buzzing with the chatter of excited visitors as the trains rolled in one after the other. Most of the visitors came from the industrial towns of the East Midlands, but many came from Lincoln itself – so many that, for a time, some liked to call Skegness 'Lincoln-by-the-Sea'. Others came from further afield including the metropolis itself – there was a group of 80 on a staff trip from the North London Railway.

Some 30 of the railway workers made their way to the beach and began looking about for something to do. They

9

saw some fishermen who were offering to take people out for boat trips, and it was agreed to make a voyage up and down the Lincolnshire coast.

The boat they selected was *The Shannon*, a vessel in which they had every reason to feel confident as it was crewed by two experienced men from the Skegness lifeboat – Edward Grunnill and William Grunnill; these two were cousins married to two sisters. The Grunnills were typical of the way in which the 'old' economy of Skegness – a fishing town – had adapted to the profits to be made from the 'new' tourist economy. Loading the excursionists aboard proved to be something of a problem as there was some 'larking about', but this was no more than was typical among excursionists and certainly not enough to have encouraged the dark rumours that were later spread about the behaviour on the boat.

Edward Grunnill took *The Shannon* out into the North Sea about three quarters of a mile from the shore, then followed along the coast until it was opposite the Vine Hotel. He was just turning the boat about for the return journey when it was struck by a sudden and vicious squall. The thunder crashed out, lightning flickered around and the rain lashed the exposed excursionists. The Grunnills immediately realised the danger as the sails were still set, and they struggled to haul them in. Their frantic efforts were to no avail for within seconds the gale dragged the boat over and it capsized, throwing everyone into the water.

One of the few who survived was George Chadburn. He could remember little, but recalled, 'The thunder and lightning were very heavy, and a powerful squall was the cause of the capsizing .. before we could get the sail down.' Chadburn denied strongly that 'larking about' on the boat had prevented its crew from getting the sail down. He had fallen into the sea wearing an overcoat and carrying a walking stick, but was a strong swimmer who had won many prizes. By waving the walking stick around he was able to attract a rescuing boat.

The disaster was witnessed by Jabez Grunnill, a relative of

The boat in this relaxed scene on the beach at Skegness is similar in type to the 'Shannon', which capsized with considerable loss of life in 1893 (Lincoln Library Local Studies Collection).

The *Shannon*'s crew. He was fishing about a mile away and saw the storm strike the pleasure boat, but there was little he could do to save its passengers. He was able to rescue three survivors from the water and picked up twelve bodies which were taken to Hildred's Hotel, where they were ticketed and laid out in an outhouse. He estimated that he had seen another seven bodies still in the water, and he saw his two cousins sink beneath the waves as he watched helplessly.

The North London Railway group had arranged an evening dinner for themselves, and this became a grim wake. Charles Odell reported that there were 27 faces missing when they met for dinner and said that he had himself refused an invitation to go on the fateful trip. Edward and William Grunnill also died, leaving a wife and seven children each.

The storm itself passed over Skegness to cause widespread devastation in the rest of Lincolnshire. Boston Stump was struck by lightning, causing a huge stone pinnacle to crash to the ground. At Spalding Marsh a bullock and a horse were killed by lightning, while at Guyhirn the landlord of The

11

Cross Guns was killed. Ten sheep were killed in the same way at Martin.

The capsized *The Shannon* was discovered two miles from the scene of the disaster. There was nothing wrong with the boat itself and it was working well within its licensed capacity of 60 passengers. However, the disaster caused a total collapse in the Skegness boating trade, which was a valuable source of extra revenue for local fishermen. A relief fund was set up for the 19 widows and 70 children affected by the disaster.

Some of the bodies were never recovered. By 21st July, eleven were still missing although three had been found in the past week including one at Hunstanton. Two had been seen in Boston Deeps but not picked up due to the tide. The relief fund was at £400, a relatively low figure considering the number affected by this terrible disaster that had struck suddenly in the midst of a pleasant summer excursion.

Sad though it was, the boat tragedy proved to be a small setback on Skegness' road to success. By 1907 it was being visited by 321,000 excursionists yet it was not until the year after this that the Great Northern Railway played a masterstroke for its captive resort – it commissioned artist John Hassall to design a publicity poster, and he came up with the famous 'Jolly Fisherman'. In 1913, perhaps the final year in the golden age of many a coastal resort, 750,000 people visited little Skegness.

Captain Swing's Ride of Terror

★

The early 1830s were a time of crisis throughout Britain. In Westminster the most powerful men in the nation were arguing over the reform of the political system and tempers were getting strained. The deadly cholera was reaching out to ensnare Britain in its clammy grasp for the first time, while in rural areas there was a new and terrifying name abroad – Captain Swing.

Captain Swing was a mythical figure, rather like Ned Ludd of the Luddites. Swing's name was used by agricultural labourers who were protesting about low wages and the threat to their jobs made by the new threshing machines. Their best weapon against recalcitrant farmers was fire – for farmers in remote areas could do little to protect their stacks and buildings and any 'fire service' was unable to help effectively. The arsonists soon discovered that the chances of them being detected were slim.

The first of the troubles broke out in Kent, spreading north from there. In November 1830 the *Boston Gazette* reported the first results of this in Lincolnshire – some insurance offices were refusing to cover agricultural property. However, for a time the local press had nothing to report except gloating stories about the troubles in Kent and Sussex – Captain Swing's journey had not yet brought him to Lincolnshire.

However in mid November 1830 the paper reported the first Swing attack in Lincolnshire with some alacrity – too much alacrity, as it turned out. There was a huge blaze on the Rev F Swan's premises at Saucethorpe, which was immediately assumed to be the work of Swing. In fact it was caused much more traditionally – a gang of small boys set light to some waste corn and the blaze got out of control.

The first genuine Swing attack seems to have been at Stickford on 24th November when a stackyard caught fire. At first it was hoped that this was a random event, the 'work of private malice unconnected with the general plan'. Whether there was a general plan is doubtful, but the Stickford blaze was followed rapidly by others at Muckton and Ireby. On 26th November a large fire did £700 damage in destroying George Mawer's stackyard at South Reston near Louth. The following day a wheat field caught fire at Swaby and two days later there was another fire near Somercoates.

Terror now struck at the hearts of Lincolnshire farmers, who felt themselves totally at the mercy of the unseen arsonist or 'incendiarist'. Conspiracy theories abounded – there was talk of suspicious strangers seen on horseback or creeping about on foot, often asking questions about the character of local farmers or whether they used threshing machines. A 'well-dressed and respectable man' stayed at

Stowegate Farm was an isolated and easy target for the Swing arsonists in the 1830s.

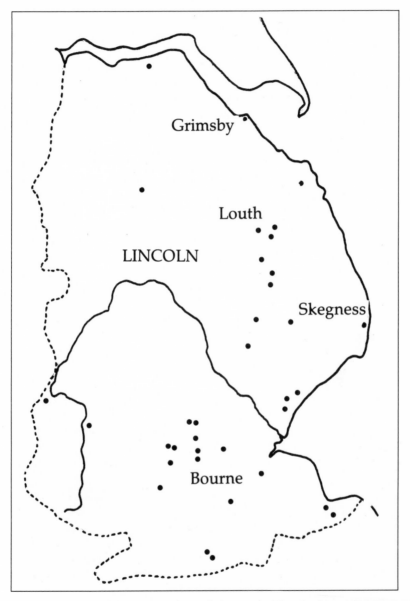

The location of Swing attacks and threats in Lincolnshire 1830-31.

the Crown Inn, Surfleet, and asked questions about local farmers – offering money for information. Such stories fuelled the fear that the Swing attacks were the work of organised revolutionaries, but there is little solid evidence to support this – most of the Swing attacks were the work of locals, paying back the grudges built up over years.

On 30th November the arsonists struck at Spalding and large numbers of special constables began to enrol in the district. At Louth a subscription of £800 was raised to fight the 'menace' but this did not stop a steady stream of threatening letters to local farmers.

One of the first arrests occurred after a fire at Sutton Marsh, near Long Sutton, on 2nd December. Two men (one of whom worked for the farmer who had been attacked) and a boy were sent to Lincoln Castle. Yet arrests were rare, despite large rewards. After a man was seen leaping over a paddock gate in Horncastle, a reward of £550 was offered to no effect; few labourers were prepared to turn against their own kind.

Few farms had the chance of being saved by the fire brigade, often because of the distance to the nearest town. On 5th December a stack of oats was saved at Market Rasen, simply because it was close enough to the town for the fire engine to get there in time.

What is clear, though, is that only certain sectors of society were interested in stopping the Swing attacks. A revealing incident occurred at Barton on 5th December. A fire broke out in two wheat stacks and one of barley that belonged to John Westoby and were about three miles outside Barton. Westoby had received a threatening letter, warning him against using threshing machines, but had ignored it; in fact he had sworn at men he thought had sent the letter. When the blaze broke out at about 6 pm, over 200 people came out from Barton to 'help', but instead 'The Barton populace that surrounded the stacks looked on with the most perfect indifference and not an expression of regret.' Even as the stacks burnt, Westoby began to smash his threshing machine to pieces.

Some farmers paid armed guards to watch over their stacks. At Donington on the night of 7th December a man attempted to set light to a stack and was shot by the guard; he ran off, leaving a trail of blood, but it was never discovered what had happened to him.

The fires continued into mid December and began to achieve their purposes. The farmers around Boston started to give in to wage demands as the best way to insure against Swing's attacks. Interestingly, one paper received a letter from Spilsby saying that there was no general conspiracy among the protesters – but a couple of weeks later received a letter saying 'strangers' were co-ordinating the attacks from 'near Spilsby'. On 10th December Swing struck at Dyke near Bourne and a threatening letter was received in Gainsborough – opening up a new area. There were also some near accidents – a farmer at Wigtoft nearly shot two bankers who seemed 'suspicious'.

As Christmas approached, there was a large fire at Belton, near Grantham; a reward of £1,330 was offered. A Scotch grazier named Clarke ran Stowegate Farm near Deeping St James, and took the precaution of employing a man and a boy to watch for attacks. Both were asleep when, the week before Christmas, Swing struck. Clarke lost property of about £2,000 to the flames – cornstacks, buildings, a threshing machine, 14 cows, four horses and two pigs. The following week there were seven fires in Lindsey. A man named Clipsham Allen was arrested for this in January 1831 but was found not guilty.

Swing hardly paused for Christmas. On Boxing Day a threshing machine was smashed at Folkingham and on 28th December £500 of damage was done by fire at Glentham. A stack was destroyed there, but Mr Thorpe's house was saved by the arrival of the Market Rasen fire engine and his cows were rescued by a passer-by. A vagrant from Louth was arrested but most people believed the fire was the work of a local man. This incident led several local parishes to discuss whether they should buy their own fire engine.

The old year was seen out with stack fires at Heckington

and Pointon on 30th December. The Pointon fire involved a stack that had recently been threshed by machine and was put out with the help of 27 men from Dowsby, who were given a shilling each and some bread and cheese for their trouble. During the operation, a bucket fell from the stack onto the head of a Mr Sydney; he was treated promptly by a doctor by being 'profusely bled'.

On 9th December 1830 a man named Lunn from Great Hale sent a letter to farmer William Green, who seems to have been involved with the overseers of the poor. The letter, posted in Sleaford, read:

'Mr Green – as sure as you are a bad man, you may expect a visit before Christmas. If you do not let the poor have all the coals together this year, you shall have a bullet. Bread or blood, my boys, fire or smoke.'

Lunn was arrested after Christmas and sentenced to 18 months hard labour. The phrases at the end of the letter were typical Swing slogans.

The authorities also came down savagely on anyone who tried to organise the workers to get higher wages. In January three Heckington men were given three months prison each for unlawful assembly after organising a meeting on the green to demand wage increases. The women also got involved – Lucy Trollope sent a note round the women of Heckington to meet outside Mr Almond's bakery in order to force him to sell bread at lower prices; she was given three months hard labour for riotous assembly.

By late January the authorities were making progress with arrests becoming more regular. Men were taken into custody for sending threatening letters to farmers around Folkingham and at Baumber. The latter was given six months in prison.

Mr Thorpe of Owersby near Market Rasen caught a Swing agent by clever detective work. In early February he received a threatening letter, but thought no more of it. He later sent a man to buy a ton of hay and asked him to bring a receipt.

The receipt was written on a scrap of torn paper and Thorpe recognised the writing – and the tear of the paper allowed him to match it exactly to the threatening letter! The author, a 'loose character', was sent to Kirton gaol.

By March 1831 the trouble seemed to be subsiding. This was because much farm work was seasonal and with the arrival of the spring there were fewer people without work. One of the reasons the threshing machine was so detested was that it replaced one of the traditional winter jobs that gave men some certainty of year-round work. For a while, at least, Lincolnshire farmers were careful how they treated their labourers; though Swing faded away, the threat of fire remained until the end of the century as a means of retribution.

Of the many arrested, only Thomas Mottley and Richard Cooling paid the ultimate price on 29th July 1831. They were executed for fires in the Hagnaby and Kirkby districts.

The Baby Farmers

★

Lincolnshire is famous as a farming county and its agricultural produce, from potatoes to pork pies, is known throughout the country. It is curious, then, that the county hit the headlines in 1907 for a different sort of farming altogether – baby farming.

Baby farming was a practice more associated with the 19th century than the 20th, but in the Edwardian era there were still a few practices that harked back to the bad old days. It was an age when illegitimate children were remarkably common and yet a major impediment to a young woman's progress – a single woman with a child found it hard to get somewhere to live, to get a decent job and to get a husband. Therefore there were many dubious people who offered to 'look after' unwanted babies, and the little ones were thus 'farmed out' to whoever would take them for a few shillings a week.

Early in 1907 an apparently innocent advertisement appeared in a Lincolnshire paper: 'Young couple in comfortable circumstances have good home for a child.'

The advert was seen by a pregnant single woman in Grimsby, Lily Kitching. Lily discussed the matter with her mother and they decided that the advert might be a solution to their problem – an unwanted child. The advert stipulated that the couple wanted to adopt a baby as a final solution, not just to look after one or foster it. It also requested a 'premium' of £15 in order to cover their initial costs; this should have been a warning to Lily, but she was desperate to sort out her affairs.

Lily wrote to a Mr J Baker at an address in Liverpool. Baker replied on impressive monogrammed paper, saying that he and his wife would take the baby and that they would only require a premium of £11. Within a few days Lily received a telegram telling her that Mr Baker would be coming to Grimsby with his wife, and shortly afterwards the couple turned up at Lily's mother's house. Baker told the grandmother that his wife was unable to have children, and the couple took the baby and the money away with them – it was then just two weeks old. The man also said that he and his wife were setting up home in Bristol and Lily was welcome to visit them there; in the meantime, they were holidaying near Liverpool.

No doubt Lily thought that was an end of the matter, but two days later she received a letter from Baker asking for £2 to cover the train fare to Grimsby and another £5 to 'settle the account'. The letter was postmarked New Brighton, which seemed to fit in with the story of them being on holiday – though it would seem strange to go on holiday while adopting a baby.

Lily's mother began to be worried and decided to go to Liverpool to see Baker herself. However, she found that the address he had given her was a 'letter call office' and began to have terrible fears. Perhaps the Bakers had taken the money and killed the baby? She went straight to the nearest police station and told her story. The police were able to arrest the 'Bakers' – in reality Herbert Smith and Lottie Roberts. They were charged with having caused the death of the baby and having obtained money by false pretences.

The case caused a sensation in Lincolnshire, which was added to by the strange revelations about the 'farmers'. Smith, aged 21, was a music hall artiste famous for escapology including the undoing of handcuffs. Lottie Roberts was his lover who had herself had an unwanted baby.

While Smith and Roberts were being held in custody, the news was released that the missing baby had been found – farmed out in Lincoln! After meeting Lily and her mother, the couple had travelled straight to Lincoln by train where they had given the baby to another woman to look after. This woman had been contacted by advertising for someone to look after a baby. She had been paid the first two weeks' money in advance, but had never heard from the 'parents' again. The woman had then dumped the baby into the nearest workhouse.

The charge of causing a baby's death was dropped, but further revelations came out. A Mrs S Frith from Branston near Lincoln came forward to say that she had been looking after a baby boy and that she suspected Smith and Roberts had farmed it out to her. She said that she had seen an advert in the newspaper in April, in which a Mr and Mrs Smith from Liverpool had asked for people to look after a baby for a few shillings a week. She had written off to them and a few days later received a telegram telling her to meet them at Lincoln station.

Mrs Frith had met the couple on the platform and was able to identify them later as Smith and Roberts. Mrs Frith and Roberts had gone into the waiting room to discuss arrangements for the baby, which was about two weeks old at the time. Whether or not this was the same baby that Lily Kitching had handed over in Grimsby is impossible to say with certainty, but it seems more likely that it had come from Sheffield as that is where Smith had sent the telegram from.

Mrs Frith and Roberts agreed that the baby should be looked after for 5s 6d a week, with 11s being paid in advance. Roberts and Smith then went off by train, but Mrs Frith never heard from them again – nor did she receive any money.

Smith and Roberts managed to juggle a whole series of babies, though why they seemed so interested in the Lincoln area is a mystery. The probability is that once they had obtained one contact in a place, they advertised both for babies and 'adoptive mothers' in the local press so as to get the maximum profit out of their train fare. The week after Mrs Frith's revelations it was learnt that a Lincoln woman had answered a local press advert and had handed her baby over to a woman in Altrincham, together with £15. Another advert in a Lincoln paper led to a local woman 'adopting' a baby at a rate of 3s 6d a week – clearly a less astute businesswoman than Mrs Frith. There was a strong possibility that this was the same baby going to and fro across the country.

In June 1907 Smith and Roberts appeared in court charged with five offences of taking money under false pretences. They had run a slick marketing campaign with a remarkable turnover of babies, but admitted their offences in court. They had made efficient use of their train fares, shuttling between one mother and a 'farmer' and then to another mother. A baby collected in Lincoln was taken to St Pancras in London, where they had collected another baby and taken it to Sheffield. There they collected Mrs Frith's baby and took it back to Lincoln.

Smith confirmed that they had collected a baby in Altrincham and taken it back to Lincoln and he also said that they had collected one in Chester and disposed of it in Halifax within four hours. Lily Kitching's baby had been 'negotiated' even before it had been born.

Between January and June 1907 the couple dealt with about 20 babies, many of them in Lincolnshire. They collected about £200 for this, most of which was profit; five of the babies brought in £66 for a total outlay of only £3!

In his defence, Smith said that they had had a baby themselves and had advertised for someone to look after it. The response had been so great that they had been given the idea for their deception. He assured the court that the babies never came to any harm and that most ended up in the workhouse. He also told the court that he had saved a young woman in Bristol from suicide by helping to arrange a 'home' for her baby. The court sentenced Smith to 15 months in prison and Roberts to eight months. The reason for their choosing Lincoln station as a convenient place for dealing in babies was never explained.

The Lion and the Prostitutes' Padre

★

The summer season at Skegness amusement park in 1937 included an unusual and very popular attraction – a disgraced clergyman performing a lion taming act. Sadly, this led to one of the most bizarre tragedies that Lincolnshire has ever seen.

On that balmy summer evening, 62 year old Harold Davidson had prepared for his act as a crowd of over 200 spectators gathered. Many of them were encouraged to pay their money because of the weird spectacle of Davidson being in such a situation – he had become notorious as the 'Prostitutes' Padre' and had been forced from his living at Stiffkey in Norfolk due to an overzealous interest in fallen women. As the *Chronicle*'s 'X-Ray' column later remarked 'What attracted the public was seeing a former much-reported figure in a bizarre setting.'

What had brought Davidson to such a sorry fate? From an early age it had been intended that he should enter the Church, but he also had an interest in the stage and showmanship seems to have been a powerful part of his character. Once in the Church, he gained an incumbency at Stiffkey which yielded him a handsome salary, but he maintained an interest in London actresses – making a nuisance of himself in their dressing rooms.

He spent time as a military chaplain during the Great War and was once arrested in a Cairo brothel. On his return, he discovered that his wife was pregnant by someone else and abandoned any pretence of a normal home life. Davidson spent most of his time in London, looking for young women who he could 'help' – usually by offering to get them jobs

24

on the stage. Some of the girls were brought back to Stiffkey though Davidson neglected such basic parochial duties as turning up on time for church services.

In 1925 he was declared bankrupt after becoming involved with a confidence trickster. Then a local magistrate, Major Philip Hammond, decided to complain to the Bishop of Norwich about Davidson's slackness and the scandal of his involvement with loose women. By December 1931 the Bishop had accumulated enough evidence from a private detective to convince him of the need to act – he proposed that Davidson resign his living. Davidson decided to fight and one of his first moves was to try and use the press to put pressure on the Bishop, who was afraid of the scandal.

In March 1929 Davidson was called before a Church consistory court, though he remained confident in his own cause and, indeed, still retained the support of many local people. Though the evidence given by many actresses and prostitutes was unconvincing, Davidson had a difficult time when giving evidence himself. The prosecution was able to produce a photograph of him posing with a semi-naked 15 year old girl, and Davidson's attempted explanations were

The Rev Harold Davidson with some of his female friends. His relationships with 'loose women' eventually led to his expulsion from the priesthood.

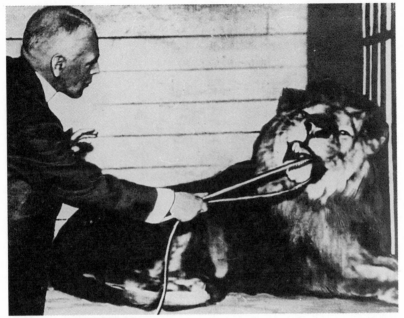

Rev Davidson apparently in the Lion's Den. His lion-taming act was finally to bring tragedy in 1937.

plainly unconvincing. In July 1932 he was found guilty of immoral conduct and in October was 'defrocked' at Norwich Cathedral.

Davidson reverted to his interest in showmanship, spending five years as a sideshow attraction in Blackpool. However, the public's interest in him declined and it was the desperate need of employment and a platform for his continued protestation of innocence that led him to work in the lions' den at Skegness.

Davidson's show was billed as a re-creation of Daniel in the Lions' Den. Each performance involved him walking amongst the lions, doing some rudimentary tricks with them, and then making a speech about his misfortunes. On the fatal evening, Davidson seems to have knocked against a young lioness, Toto, as she was making her entrance to the arena. The lioness's mate, Freddie, took this as some form of

26

attack and pounced on Davidson. At first the audience took this to be part of the show, but their laughs turned to screams as the savagery of the lion's attack became apparent. Many fled in terror, leaving Davidson to his fate.

Davidson tried to fight Freddie off, but the lion pushed him to the floor and clawed at his shoulders, neck and back. The errant clergyman screamed for help and his cries were answered by a brave young woman of 16 named Miss Irene Summers (or Somner), who was a lion tamer with 'Captain Rye's forest-bred lion troupe'.

The young woman grabbed a whip and rushed into the cage. She beat Freddie back off Davidson and into a corner, allowing just enough time for attendants to rush in and drag the mortally wounded man away. As others came to help, Miss Summers collapsed – but she can be seen as the true heroine of the hour.

Davidson was taken to Skegness Cottage Hospital, but he was badly wounded and had a broken neck. His wife and daughters were called from London but he died on 30th July, protesting his innocence until the end. His death from the claws of the lion can be directly attributed to the earlier events of his life, for he seems to have taken to the sport of lion taming as a way of attracting attention to his cause. He was always looking for opportunities to give lectures on his life and was trying to arrange one for Lincoln at the time of his death.

The Diamond Jubilee

★

The 22nd June 1897 was a great day throughout the British Empire – it was the Diamond Jubilee of Queen Victoria. After beginning her reign more than half a century before as a shy young girl, she had grown into a strong monarch before the death of Albert had turned her into a recluse. As the never-smiling, drably dressed 'widow of Windsor', Victoria had gone through a period of unpopularity before being coaxed back into society by the flamboyant and romantic Disraeli, who dreamt up her grandest title – Empress of India. Thus she survived to be the beloved old lady whose achievements were celebrated throughout her Empire and nowhere with greater enthusiasm than in the streets and halls of Lincolnshire.

Preparations for the celebrations began several months earlier. The Mayor of Lincoln received a royal command to appear at Buckingham Palace on the great day. He ensured that this got maximum publicity, and the press was fed copious details on the outfit he would be wearing – a cocked hat, mulberry coat, white waistcoat, trousers trimmed with gold lace and a sword at his side.

The Lincoln Board of Poor Law Guardians' preparations were rather more prosaic. Meeting several weeks in advance, they accepted the offer of Mr Danby to use his house and gardens to entertain the paupers. They also accepted the offer of Mr Hatton to lay on food at 1s 6d per head – this was to include mutton, beef, pies, pickles, rolls, cheese, plum bread, seed bread, pastry and cakes. A benefactor gave 18 gallons of beer to wash it all down with. The Guardians also decided to hire the Malleable Ironworks Brass Band as it would cost 'very little indeed'. It was agreed that an evening 'spectacle' should be organised by the

Labour Master. The *Lincolnshire Chronicle* headlined this report, 'An Earthly Paradise'.

More importantly, perhaps, a collection was organised to provide some permanent memorial to the Queen. Lincoln people collected £4,000 which was used to endow Miss Bromhead's Nursing Home. The people of Boston collected £2,000 to set up a Free Library and add to the hospital, while in Grantham a new font cover was bought for St Wulfram's. Brigg subscribed £110 to its local Nursing Association. In Skegness, money was collected for a Jubilee Clock Tower, but it was another two years before this was opened officially.

On Sunday 20th June a huge thanksgiving service was held at Lincoln Cathedral, with music from 400 choristers. The songs included one that would probably be considered too nationalistic for today's sensibilities:

'Where England's flag flies wide unfurled
All tyrant wrongs repelling,
God makes the world a better world
For man's brief earthly dwelling.'

Boston also organised a service on the Sunday which was attended by about 3,000 people. Among those present were the Mayor and Corporation, the bands of the Rifle Volunteers and Artillery, the fire brigade and the police. The Stump could also claim the most exotic preacher that day – the Bishop of Rockhampton, Australia. In the afternoon there was a flower service for children, attended by about a thousand.

In Brigg there were also Sunday services and in the afternoon children met in the Market Place to sing.

Grantham got its main celebrations off to an early start by beginning on Monday 21st June. A reception was held in the Guildhall for 400 select locals, with entertainment by the Albertini Band and a Nottingham conjurer. Also off to an early start was the village of Morton where the Conservative candidate for Gainsborough, Edward Pearson, gave a tea for

350 at Morton Hall. Cigars and ale were given out to the men.

On Jubilee Day itself, Tuesday 22nd June, Lincolnshire's celebrations focused on the County Town, especially for people from the surrounding villages. Early that morning people were already pouring into the city, and continued to do so throughout the day. Celebrations began when a procession formed up outside the Central station behind the band of the Lincoln Volunteers. The procession then marched through the city to the cathedral, where a service was held for invited people only. Rumours were later rife that the service had been disrupted by a 'socialistic display', but this turned out to have only been a man waving a handkerchief. After the service, the procession marched back to the station.

In the afternoon athletic and bicycle sports were held on the West Common and the city's children, about 12,000 of them, were given tea.

Yet the real interest was in the evening events which included an aquatic display on the Brayford Pool and the decoration of many central buildings with lights. Huge crowds toured the streets, enjoying the spectacle of Christmas effects in the middle of summer. The Constitutional Club looked like 'a fairy palace', the Cornhill Hotel was bedecked with Japanese lanterns, the Black Bull with green houseplants and all the shops in similar style. Prizes were given for the best effort: first prize went to Fox & Co in the High Street where even the roof was covered with flowers, while the front of the shop was dressed in lamps and palms – the windows were filled with mirrors, with lamps placed in front of them to dazzling effect. The Stonebow was decorated with 2,500 fairy lamps and 500 coloured gas lamps while the Obelisk on High Bridge and the Conduit were also lit. According to the *Chronicle,* there was 'only one dull place in the city and that was the Liberal Club.' However, one shouldn't always trust a newspaper – especially, in this instance, a Conservative one!

Most interesting of all, however, was the cathedral. Messrs

The Stonebow in Lincoln decorated for Queen Victoria's Diamond Jubilee in 1897. (Lincoln City Library Local Studies Collection)

31

Robeys had provided 42 arc lamps which were driven by a dynamo placed in the Dean's Garden and at 10pm a rocket was fired from the cathedral's central tower as a signal for bonfires to be lit throughout the county. By the end of the evening it was possible to see 30 bonfires from the tower, including ones as far away as the Vale of Belvoir.

One of the first bonfires to be lit was a huge one at Cross o' Cliff Hill. This was 60ft around and 15ft high and fuelled by materials given by local firms. Sadly, sports at the site were disrupted by unruly drunkards and 'caddish behaviour'.

Events in other places around the county suffered by comparison. Boston had a 60 gun salute but other rejoicings were 'modest'. The Post Office employees sang the National Anthem and sent a telegram to the Queen while at 12.30pm 600 aged poor were given a free dinner in the Corn Exchange. In the afternoon 6,000 children gathered in the Market Place to sing the National Anthem with tea given afterwards. The day ended with a torchlight procession with tar barrels and the town's bonfire was lit on Bargate Common.

Brigg probably had the most unusual celebrations and right from the outset its streets had 'a very festive appearance'. Its unique feature was in holding the main celebrations on water, starting at 10am with a water pageant of pretty boats along the river and round the island. The Chairman of Brigg UDC voyaged intrepidly in a steam gondola named *Stanley*, returning safely to speak from the balcony of the Angel Hotel. One hundred and fifty aged poor were rustled up for dinner and 750 children had tea in a tent behind the Manor House. The workhouse inmates were fed beef and plum pudding while there were sports and fireworks in the evening.

Grantham had 'shot the bolt' the previous day, but began with two hours of bell ringing at 8am. Seven hundred of the aged poor had their dinner, consuming 370lbs of beef, 200lbs of mutton, 64lbs of ham, 200lbs of plum pudding, 34 stones of potatoes, 700 pints of beer and 40 loaves of bread. Some

4,260 children packed into the Market Place to sing but most interest was attracted to the Barracks field where displays were laid on in the evening featuring Miss Dora the trapeze artist and the Zetina acrobats. The evening was marred when a horse and cart, left in the charge of a small boy, bolted and several people were injured. This did not stop the torchlight procession to Hall's Hill where a 30ft high bonfire was lit.

Gainsborough did nothing for its reputation – it was reckoned to be one of the most boring places for the Diamond Jubilee. There was a gala on the cricket field with a cycle parade and 'old English' sports. It was hoped to collect enough money to abolish the toll on the bridge. Grimsby people fared little better – a new chiming clock was dedicated at the church and in the evening there was an outdoor magic lantern display at the town hall.

The people of Louth dedicated a new piece of public open space in Upgate and organised an artillery salute. There was the usual assembly of singing children, each bribed with a piece of Jubilee cake. A huge bonfire was lit at the London toll-bar.

Sleaford's procession was headed by the Nottingham Sax Tuba Brass Band and the local Drum & Fife Band. There was a fancy dress cycle parade in the evening and the regulation huge bonfire – reckoned to be 50ft high. The people of Bourne did much the same thing, though they could only manage a 20ft bonfire.

The people of Spalding sent a telegram to the Queen and gave a meal to old people with 'lavishly spread and profusely decorated tables'.

Perhaps the character of the county can best be seen in the way the Jubilee was celebrated in its smaller settlements. At Scotter there was a unique and historical event – the Anglicans and the Nonconformists held a joint service in the parish church with a total of four clergymen in attendance. Market Rasen staged a cycle parade with 'novel, grotesque and beautiful figures'; the lights of Lincoln could just be seen from the town. At Stainfield, a tiny village, the children were given 6d each whilst the benefits of ringing the bells at Stow must have seemed doubtful – they began at 5am! The children of Normanby and Owmby were each given an orange while at Wrangle the whole village sat down to a free tea paid for by the local subscription of £36 – unfortunately it rained. The Washingborough villagers took the opportunity of organising a cycle parade that invaded the streets of the despised neighbours in Heighington. At Bucknall the landowners gave all tenants and labourers a plum loaf, tobacco and a bottle of wine while the children at Halton Holgate got a Jubilee mug each.

Celebrations continued for days afterwards, usually in descending order of importance. Thus on 23rd June it was the turn of Lincoln's aged poor, 1,200 of whom had tea in the Drill Hall and Corn Exchange. The following day the workhouse paupers got their turn – after the feast there was a 'spectacle', involving a play about a raid on an African travelling party with the workhouse boys playing the natives.

As far as is known, the celebrations cost only two lives. At 2.15am on 23rd June a young man decided to go swimming in the Fosse dyke at Lincoln and drowned, while another man died at the Lock Tavern after jumping into the water for no apparent reason at all.

Altogether the Jubilee celebrations provide a fascinating snapshot of a period when Lincolnshire towns rivalled each other in constructing the biggest bonfires and when 'fairy lights' were a major attraction for thousands. What is most curious is how fashions change – who would now think of celebrating anything with a cycle parade?

Stop the Wedding!

★

Falling in love in Victorian England was a serious business – in particular for young people with middle class parents. And getting married was far more complicated than it is today. One reason for this was that any couple who did not come from the labouring class was liable to undergo a sort of 'means test' from their parents. Did the man have the means to support the lady in the style to which she was accustomed? Indeed, to what style *was* she accustomed? What sort of family did each come from? The answer 'We are simply in love with each other' was not a response that could be sensibly entertained.

For two sweethearts of this category such attitudes could lead to frustration and disappointment. Occasionally, they were forced to do something desperate . . .

In the summer of 1851 there was no more loving couple in the whole of Lincolnshire than Frederick Sharpe and Elizabeth Lunn. Frederick was a joiner, the son of a respectable widowed lady from Washingborough. His true love Elizabeth was one of the twin daughters of the late Mr R Lunn, proprietor of the White Swan Inn in Lincoln – more commonly known as the 'Pig and Whistle'.

The fact that the inn had an official name and a popular name is perhaps a clue as to why Frederick ran into problems in his bid to win the hand of the fair Elizabeth. Clearly Mrs Lunn saw herself as responsible for an establishment that was a cut above the standard of a beer-shop. And no doubt Mrs Lunn (who since Mr Lunn's death had found herself another husband, Mr Burnham) fancied that her family was a level above the vulgar as well. Poor Frederick Sharpe seems to have been classed with the vulgar in her eyes.

The two had met in 1848 when Frederick was 18 and an

apprentice to a Lincoln building firm. 'Mama' Lunn had taken an instant dislike to him, and had launched her counter-attack by packing both her daughters off to Manchester. Sadly for her, this strategy had no effect as Frederick learnt where Elizabeth had gone and even managed to visit her there.

They kept in touch through letters, going as far as to start planning how they could get married. However, the loving correspondence was intercepted on 'Mama's' instructions. Undaunted, Elizabeth made new arrangements for letters to be sent via a friend.

This ruse though, proved to Mrs Lunn that her Manchester plan was not working, and she brought her daughters back to Lincoln. For a while Elizabeth was totally confined to the house through the very simple scheme of keeping all her outdoor clothes locked up; in fact some people even said that Elizabeth herself was locked up too. There was no sign of any more letters, so her mother began to relax, thinking that the youthful passion had spent itself. She was wrong.

Sadly for her, but happily for Cupid, romance was still very much alive. One Saturday night Frederick Sharpe returned to Lincoln by a late train. He took care not to be seen about the streets and visited only close and trustworthy friends. With these friends he was able to arrange a special licence for a marriage on the Monday morning. His friends also helped to spirit away Elizabeth's best clothes from the house that had become her prison.

That fateful weekend Mrs Lunn's new husband, Mr Burnham, was away at the Great Exhibition in London. Mrs Lunn, being a Victorian lady of sensitive disposition, did not like to sleep alone and so on the Sunday night she retired to bed with her other daughter – leaving Elizabeth quite alone. The lovestruck girl somehow slipped out of the house and spent the rest of the night in lodgings that had been arranged for her near St Botolph's church.

It was but a short step from the lodgings to the church, where Reverend Jepson married the young couple first thing in the morning. Then, with joy in their hearts, the new Mr and Mrs Sharpe took a 'fly' to Washingborough, while her family still believed that she (as Miss Elizabeth Lunn) was asleep in her room at the 'Pig and Whistle'.

The first that her mother learned of events was when a friend came to the inn to tell her the story that was doing the rounds. Her fury can be imagined. She made straight for the station to catch the first train to Washingborough, reckoning that the young couple would have gone to see the groom's mother, Mrs Sharpe. Mrs Lunn made it clear to everyone who knew about the affair that she was going 'to put a stop to it'.

Flushed and almost speechless with indignation, she arrived at Frederick's family home which was in a state of high festivity. She demanded to see her daughter. We can imagine her feelings when she was informed that her daughter did not wish to see her! Mrs Lunn had to be content with a glimpse of the happy groom and his best friend, who had done most of the arranging. He was rewarded for his efforts by the bride's mother calling him 'a villain and a ringleader'. Her abuse and shouting was such that she missed the last train and had to walk three miles home at night.

This walk home was the cause of the last fateful twist in the story for the frustrated lady. Along the lane she met a reporter for the *Stamford Mercury*, a man who had had his ear to the ground and knew something of what had been going on. He had no trouble identifying the flustered and excitable figure of the bride's mother. Mrs Lunn immediately instructed the young reporter that he was not to put a word of the story in the newspaper, thereby ensuring the man's determination to make a good story of it.

Mrs Lunn would have no truck with him; she said that she would write directly to the editor about his behaviour. The reporter replied, 'You may write to the Devil if you like.'

'That will amount to much the same thing,' she stormed, thus providing the editor of the *Stamford Mercury* with a superb story.

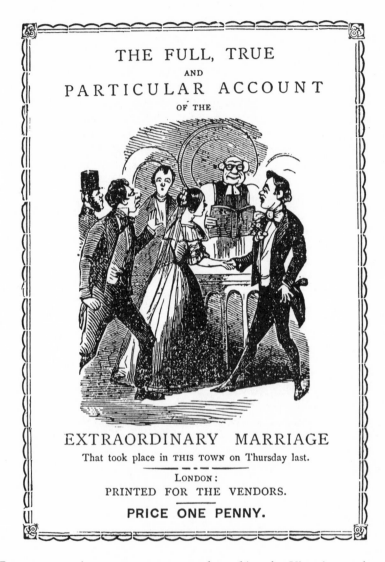

THE FULL, TRUE
AND
PARTICULAR ACCOUNT
OF THE

EXTRAORDINARY MARRIAGE
That took place in THIS TOWN on Thursday last.

LONDON:
PRINTED FOR THE VENDORS.

PRICE ONE PENNY.

Runaway marriages were a very popular subject for Victorian readers. This London broadsheet depicts a situation similar to the one at Lincoln in 1851.

Since Elizabeth was over 21, there was little her mother could do to prevent what had already been accomplished. She made do by calling on Rev Jepson to give him a stern lecture on the canon law of the Church of England. After that she gradually cooled down.

Frederick and Elizabeth Sharpe were lucky. And in the days before newspapers took wedding photographs, the young couple also achieved the best coverage of their wedding that could possibly have been expected!

Elopements, though rare, did occur several times in the period. In the 1840s, just after the opening of the Midland Railway, a couple ran away by train but they were caught at Newark by the use of the electric telegraph after the worried parents had sent a message down the line from Lincoln. Another couple eloped to Liverpool, chased by the bride's brother, who arrived just in time to offer the young couple his congratulations. No doubt there were many others who would have liked to have copied their example, but were cruelly bound by the conventions of the period.

The Trials of Thomas Bacon

★

One hundred and forty years ago, Victorian Lincolnshire was scandalised by revelations and rumours about a young man from Stamford. Greed, poison, murder and the exhumation of a corpse kept the county spellbound for months.

Thomas and Martha Bacon were a young couple from Stamford who, like many others in Victorian times, took the road to London, where they soon settled into a house in Walworth.

On the evening of 29th December 1856 Hannah Munro, Bacon's cousin, called at the house in Walworth but received no reply. This was unusual, for the Bacons were rarely away, so Hannah returned the next night – to discover Martha Bacon in a hysterically deranged state. Martha had suffered during the birth of her second child and had since shown signs of violence, but now she gasped out a story about a man getting into the house and trying to rob her. Hannah could see scratch marks on Mrs Bacon's throat and feared for the children. A few seconds later she found Edwin and Sarah both dead, their throats cut with a single vicious stroke.

The police began by assuming that Martha had gone mad and killed the children during the absence of her husband. However, they became suspicious at the story of a break-in, especially as bank notes claimed to have been stolen had all been 'passed' several weeks earlier. When Thomas Bacon himself turned up, he was found to have a cut on his right hand for which he offered conflicting explanations. Then a watch, said to have been stolen by the murderous robber, turned up on a doorstep only a quarter of a mile away – strangely careless behaviour for a desperate criminal.

Martha Bacon was brought before Lambeth magistrates on a charge of murder. Unable to speak, she handed in a written note which caused a sensation in the court:

'Sir – I must confess I am an innocent person, and he who committed the deed is my husband, and there was no money in the drawers. He took the little boy downstairs, put him in a chair, and there cut his throat. He then went upstairs and cut the baby's throat.'

Thomas Bacon, who had been watching, collapsed. He was taken to a nearby police station and charged with murder, while a crowd gathered outside to bay for his blood.

Bacon's case received a number of immediate setbacks. Firstly one of the 'stolen' banknotes was traced to Bacon's own brother, and then came some sensational news from Lincolnshire. It was reported that a few months before the family had left for London, Martha Bacon had been committed to a lunatic asylum; Bacon himself had lived with the family and a female servant at a house in Peter Hill, Stamford, until it suddenly caught fire. Although the maid helped to rescue the children from the blaze, both she and Bacon had been charged with arson. However, Bacon's trial had ended in an acquittal.

The police went to Bacon's uncle's house in Mile End, where he had been living since the murders; they found a pair of bloodstained trousers. Mrs Bacon now alleged that her husband had killed the children at 6am on 29th December, and had attacked her too – explaining the marks on her throat. Persistent rumours alleged that Bacon had also poisoned his mother before he had left Stamford.

A London officer was sent to Lincolnshire to investigate. There were plenty of rumours to go on – after his father's funeral in October 1854, Bacon had apparently said, 'There is now only the old woman's death to pray for.' More reliable evidence, though, was that Bacon had bought arsenic from a chemist's shop in Red Lion Square on 8th May 1855. Five days later the wealthy old woman, who owned several properties, had dined at Bacon's house and developed acute stomach pains which soon turned to vomiting.

The old lady had soon died but no charges had been brought against Bacon. He seems to have been very unpopular in Stamford, and many had muttered at the time that he had poisoned his mother to ensure a steady income from her estate for himself. He was also disliked for living in adultery with the maid while his wife was in the asylum and for having cheated the gas company by fixing a pipe directly into the service main, bypassing the meter at his house in Broad Street, Stamford.

The grave of Thomas Bacon's parents, Nathaniel and Ann, lies in Great Casterton churchyard. Ann's body was exhumed and found to contain traces of arsenic.

News of the Lincolnshire investigations seeped through to London only slowly, and the *Observer* complained of the 'extraordinary apathy' of the Stamford authorities. On 6th February 1857 a jury was assembled at the Plough Inn, Great Casterton, to witness the exhumation of Mrs Bacon's corpse and the examination of it by the eminent Professor Taylor. Taylor made his study in a nearby barn, and found arsenic in many organs of the body.

Revelations, rumours and clues came in profusion. Stories were told of the old lady 'twitching' before she died, then it was reported in some papers that Martha had confessed to poisoning her mother-in-law's soup while her husband had laced her medicine. Other papers just reported that Martha had confessed to the poisoning. The gaoler at Horsemonger Lane stated that Martha's neck wounds were probably self-inflicted with a rope. In mid February the Stamford coroner recorded a verdict of Wilful Murder in the case of old Mrs Bacon, naming the son as the criminal.

On 18th March Thomas Bacon appeared before Lambeth magistrates in tears. A girl described washing his shirt and finding it smeared with blood. She also said that she'd heard him say, 'Good God, how was it I done it?' Thomas and Martha Bacon were tried in May 1857 for the murder of the children. Mrs Bacon was found guilty of their murder while insane, having been in St Luke's Asylum until the October before the murders. This seemed a remarkable escape for Thomas Bacon, who was acquitted despite much opinion to the contrary; however, he was still not a free man since he had to stand trial at Lincoln for the murder of his mother.

Opinion in Lincoln was divided. There was clear evidence from Professor Taylor that Mrs Bacon had arsenic in her body, it was known that Thomas Bacon was a disreputable character and he also had a motive – with the old lady dead, he gained the income from the 18 properties she rented out in the Stamford district. However, the case against him had been steadily undermined by newspapers like the *Observer*, which had reported a statement from Bacon's wife that she had poisoned her mother-in-law without her husband's

The Plough Inn at Great Casterton was the scene of the inquest on Ann Bacon in February 1857. It was common for local inns to be used for inquest proceedings, as they were often the only public meeting places in the vicinity.

knowledge. The trial, in late July 1857, took place before Justice Erle. At first Bacon 'appeared firm and in good spirits', but later he wept often.

The charge of Wilful Murder was dropped as so long had elapsed since the death of Mrs Bacon that it was impossible to say whether she had actually been killed by the arsenic or some other cause. Instead Bacon faced a charge of administering poison with intent to murder. Much of the evidence centred on whether Bacon had needed to buy arsenic to kill rats – several witnesses believed that there had never been rats in his house.

It took the jury only ten minutes to find Bacon guilty. The judge argued that Martha Bacon could not have been the guilty person since it was her husband that bought the arsenic, but though he passed a sentence of death he also stated that 'although your guilt of the murder is established

44

beyond doubt, the extreme penalty of the law will not be carried out.'

So Bacon survived his second murder trial, but the controversy survived for some time. *The Times* continued to hint that the mad Mrs Bacon could have been the poisoner and it is one of the most intriguing aspects of this case that convincing arguments could be put forward for either of them having committed all of the murders. Perhaps we will never really know the true story of this infamous Lincolnshire couple.

Royalty Comes
to Immingham

★

In July 1912 King George V and his Queen boarded the Royal
Train at King's Cross and journeyed to north Lincolnshire in
order to open the new dock at Immingham. The programme
for the day – which the King no doubt read avidly as the
train trundled through Spalding and Boston – foretold that
'the rise of this new dock will be told as one of the romances
of Industrial England.' And thus, for a brief moment in a
millenium or two, Immingham came to be ranked as one of
the romantic sights of Britain.

Immingham's rise to fame was due to the ambitions of the
Great Central Railway which, having built itself a new main
line to London, looked to improve its facilities on the east
coast. In 1901 it selected Grimsby as the site for new docks
but because of a lack of deep water there, Sir John Wolfe
Barry convinced the company that Immingham would be
preferable. In July 1904 an Act was passed authorising new
railways and docks at Immingham, and this was to
transform the north Lincolnshire coast. At the time the area
presented 'a pastoral scene with green lanes and marshy
meadows divided by reed-filled ditches with a few copses in
the distance.'

The decision to build at Immingham caused some bad
feeling in Grimsby, to which the Earl of Yarborough was
sensitive. The GCR bought off some of the opposition by
agreeing to construct an electric light railway between the
town and the new docks.

The land was purchased from the Earl of Yarborough after
protracted negotiations and on 12th July 1906 the first sod
was cut by Lady Henderson, wife of the Great Central's

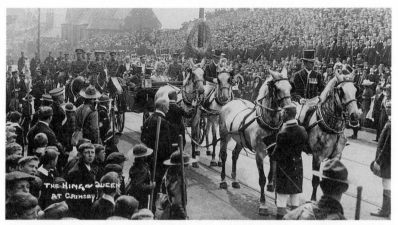

George V's drive through the streets of Grimsby in July 1912 is believed to have been seen by 100,000 people. Despite some ill feeling about the siting of the new dock at Immingham, Grimsby was determined to show its loyal support for the King. (Welholme Galleries, Grimsby)

Chairman, initiating a £2.6m project.

An army of men and their dependents arrived and up to 3,000 of them were employed in constructing the docks. Six million tons of earth had to be excavated and 700 miles of sidings laid. They were accommodated in a shanty town called Humberville, though it was also called 'Tin Town' by its denizens. Most of the buildings were of corrugated iron and timber. A dormitory accommodated about 150 men and there were 40 other huts.

The great day of the opening, to be conducted by no less a person than the King himself, was arranged for 22nd July 1912. Preparations were extensive in Grimsby and Immingham itself, for the King had agreed to make a tour of the fishing port as well. The Royal Navy arranged to have the ships *Halcyon, Leader* and *Skipjack* on station too.

The journey of the Royal Train along the East Lincolnshire line excited much interest in the county, especially in places along the route like Spalding, Boston and Louth. A Boston man named Farrow wrote to the King asking him to 'show himself' at a certain spot so that young Master Farrow, aged

47

three, would be able to see him. The King did better than this – as the train passed slowly by he saluted to the young boy and the Queen waved her handkerchief. It is impossible to imagine the security services allowing such a thing today.

Huge crowds congregated in Boston at the station and the sluice gate in order to watch the train pass through. At about noon the train passed slowly through the town, its leisurely gait being attributed to the apparent desire of the King and Queen to view Boston's famous Stump. It was reported that 'The Queen was seen at the window and King George also appeared interested in the famous tower.' The initial reception given to the Royal Train was rather muted – many people assumed that it was merely a pilot train running in advance of the main one.

The attractions of royalty nearly caused tragedy in Boston. As the train was due many of the employees at Mr Nagele's hair-net factory rushed out onto a rickety bridge between two buildings to watch. It collapsed, throwing them 24ft to the ground. Seven women and two men were injured, though the worst was only a broken leg.

The Royal Train drew into Grimsby Town station at 12.47pm for a welcoming ceremony led by Lord Heneage, the High Steward of Grimsby, but the weather was showery so they were glad that a pavilion had been erected at the station. The Mayoress presented a bouquet, made by Pennells of Lincoln, to the Queen. The royal couple then began a triumphant journey through the streets of Grimsby, during which they watched 10,000 selected schoolchildren sing the National Anthem. Estimates put the crowd that watched their progress at about 100,000. After a tour of just over a mile they got back on the train at the Docks station.

The Royal Train then took them to Immingham, where they arrived at 2.20pm in much improved weather. As it approached a specially built platform the Royal Field Artillery fired a salute. On the platform was a reception committee led by Lincolnshire's Lord Lieutenant, Lord Brownlow. This committee was at least well fed, for many of those who gathered at Immingham in advance of the King

The steamer 'Killingholme' was the first ship to enter the new dock at Immingham, with the King and Queen aboard. Thousands lined the quayside to watch.

were treated to a dinner in the No 1 transit shed – 1,418 to be precise.

The King and his party were taken aboard the steamer *Killingholme*, which was waiting outside the dock. The King pressed an electric signal, the dock gates opened, and the *Killingholme* sailed into the new port. The vessel made a 20 minute circuit of the dock amidst cheers from the crowds on the quaysides. A reception was then held in the royal pavilion, which had been placed inside No 2 transit shed. The Chairman of the GCR presented a loyal address and many speeches were made. Much of the time was spent discussing the links between royalty and the Grimsby area – Victoria had opened Grimsby's Royal Dock while the Alexandra and Union Docks had been opened by the Prince of Wales in 1879. During the course of it the King asked for a sword and unexpectedly knighted the GCR's manager, Sam Fay.

The ceremonies ended, perhaps rather blasphemously,

with a singing of 'Oh, worship the King'. The Bishop of Lincoln said a few prayers before the royal couple clambered back into the train for the journey back to London.

The idea of a port at Immingham was a good one, but war and depression prevented it ever really reaching its capacity as a coal export terminal. However, Immingham's deep water facilities made it attractive in the 1960s and 1970s as an oil terminal and, more recently, it has also handled imports of iron ore and, irony of ironies, coal. Much of this traffic is carried to and from the port by rail, thus vindicating the beliefs of the Great Central Railway. But their hopes that Immingham would feature in romantic tales have, sadly, still to bear fruit.

Death by Cough Mixture

★

Anyone who has ever looked at newspapers from the 19th century will have noticed the large numbers of advertisements dealing with all sorts of medicines. It was not until the mid Victorian period that the law began to tighten up on the myriad of quack remedies that could be bought over the counter from any untrained person who cared to set themselves up as an expert. Medicines existed for hair loss, weight gain and all manner of diseases; there were even darkly-worded adverts that hinted at mysterious ailments – by which was meant various venereal diseases.

The unofficial medical industry was gradually restricted by the passage of various laws governing the registration of doctors and pharmacists. This did not really prevent the giving of 'country' remedies and the consequent risks – in 1855 a farmer from Kelsey Bridge died after Mrs Spikins' 'infallible salve' failed to save him from septic wounds in an arm. She was arrested for manslaughter but the charges were dropped before the case reached the Assizes.

Problems continued, and the whole of the county would have been aware of the debate when a Spalding pharmacist, Atkin Gibson, was arrested for the manslaughter of Thomas Stevenson on 5th December 1902.

Stevenson was a 36 year old bachelor farmer from Surfleet Marsh. His work inevitably involved him in being outside in all weathers, and the winter of 1902 was an especially hard one for him. He caught a bad cold which persisted for more than a fortnight and so he decided to seek medical help – although he chose not to consult a doctor, which would have been expensive.

On his next trip into Spalding, accompanied by one of his labourers, Stevenson went to Atkin Gibson's pharmacy and asked for a medicine that would cure his cold. Gibson, aged 62, was not qualified in any way to practise as a chemist or pharmacist. He had begun his business in 1863 but the trade was regulated by the Pharmacy Act of 1868, which stipulated only that people setting up as chemists *after* that date had to be properly qualified. It was therefore perfectly legal for the unqualified Gibson to go into his back room to make up a medicine – but it was illegal for him to 'prescribe' it to Stevenson, since he was not a doctor and not qualified to give medical advice.

He returned from the back room with the medicine in a glass bottle. Stevenson's labourer noticed that the bottle was unusual – in fact it had previously been used as a container for a patent hair preparation! Nonetheless the farmer paid 2s to Gibson and went off with his man to The Cross Keys pub.

Both men were still in the pub at about 6pm when Stevenson took the bottle out of his pocket and decided to try some. When he opened it he noticed the strange and rather powerful smell, and several other people commented on it. A man named Spingles smelled it and said that it was very strong while another person thought that the bottle was more likely to contain sheep dressing than cough mixture! Stevenson looked at the label, which said 'One tablespoonful every four hours' and despite everyone else's advice, decided to take some. Lacking a tablespoon, he took a swig from the bottle, guessing how much to take.

The effects of Gibson's cough mixture were rapid. Within two minutes, Stevenson fell to the ground in great pain and had to be carried into the yard by his friends – suggesting that he was probably being sick as well.

The landlord, Hardwick, immediately sent for Gibson but the pharmacist needed some persuading to attend. When he arrived, Gibson's behaviour was suspicious in the extreme. He picked up the medicine bottle, poured its contents away, then put it in his pocket. He hardly seemed interested in the sick man at all and Hardwick had to argue with him to get him to look at Stevenson – by this time the farmer was prostrate with agony. Gibson agreed to give him an emetic to make him clear the poison from his system and then got ready to leave. Hardwick remonstrated with him that he should send for a doctor, but Gibson showed little interest in this suggestion.

Stevenson was taken to the Spalding hospital by his friends, but he died there at 11.50pm, the Matron commenting on the great pain he suffered. The affair rapidly became the sensation of Spalding for there would have been many others who had bought their medicine from Gibson.

The next day Inspector Melbourne visited Gibson's premises in order to retrieve as much evidence as he could. He got the bottle, but discovered that Gibson had altered the label by adding the words 'in water' after the instruction to take four spoonfuls a day. This simple attempt at deceit did no credit to Gibson's cause.

At the inquest Dr Perry reported that Stevenson's throat, stomach and intestines were 'choked up with dried mucus' due to an irritant poison. It was argued by some that Stevenson had really suffocated because the poison had destroyed all the membranes in his throat making it impossible for him to breathe. Whatever he had been given to take, it was certainly powerfully caustic – and so Gibson was arrested for manslaughter, having caused death through his own gross negligence.

Gibson's explanation was that he had made up his usual preparation for coughs and colds and had then decided to add sal volatile, which included ammonia. He said that he had mistakenly added too great a concentration of ammonia, having picked up the wrong bottle while working in his back room. The bottle he actually used and the one he should have used were four places apart on his shelves.

At the court hearing there was much discussion as to his motive in altering the label and pouring away the medicine. One wonders that discussion was necessary at all – it was clear that Gibson knew he had made a mistake and tried to cover up for himself. The court also spent time hearing how he had given Stevenson the correct emetic – acetic acid – as if this somehow atoned for his having poisoned the man in the first place.

The jury found Gibson guilty of manslaughter through negligence but various Spalding dignitaries entered pleas for mercy on his behalf. As a respected tradesman of the town, he seems to have had a number of friends. It was argued that he had already suffered in that he had had to give up his business – in fact he sold it to someone else – and that his wife had been 'stricken' by the affair. The judge decided to be lenient and sentenced Gibson to 14 days in prison, specifically without hard labour. One cannot help feeling that Stevenson's relatives would have been incensed by this decision, for the farmer had died in agony because of the carelessness of a man whose behaviour throughout the whole incident had been deplorable.

Mods and Rockers
at Skegness

★

Although the sound of The Beatles and other 'pop groups' was upsetting members of the older generation in the years 1963-4, new types of music posed relatively little physical danger to the people of Lincolnshire. Much more sinister, though, was the rise of gangs of young people who seemed to like nothing better than a good fight and were not too bothered if innocent bystanders got hurt in the ensuing melee. The gangs could be broadly divided into 'Mods' and 'Rockers', the former relying on mopeds, the latter on motorbikes.

On Bank Holiday weekends gangs of young people used to flock to coastal towns from miles around. The most publicised incidents were in Southend, Brighton and Great Yarmouth, but for the Mods and Rockers of the East Midlands the nearest available coastal town was Skegness – and not even the bracing air could keep them away.

The first real problems in Lincolnshire occurred on 17th May 1964. About 50 'leather-clad Rockers' gathered menacingly on the seafront, lining their bikes up and revving the engines in a show of strength. It seemed that they were preparing for a mass charge through the town, no doubt with consequent violence and destruction. At this point, though, the local police decided to put on a show of strength as well and for a little while the situation was tense, then the threat melted away. All the Rockers could do was shine their headlamps – not quite the orgy of debauchery and destruction that had been prophesied by the popular press.

An intrepid journalist questioned one of the Rockers, who

he described as 'a pimply-faced' youth' – though the journalist presumably did not say this at the time! The youth complained that, 'We came here looking for Mods but they are too scared to come.'

However, the Rockers did find something to do that day, a Saturday, as over 20 youths from Leicester gathered outside a public house. One youth was picked on by the Rockers and knocked to the ground, after which four of them began to hit out at him. The police moved in but there was a skirmish as the whole group tried to prevent any arrests being made. Four youths were taken into custody – one was carrying an offensive weapon in the shape of a three inch bolt with a nut on the end.

The four troublemakers were hauled up before the magistrates within three hours of being arrested. The Chairman of the magistrates, Mr Knowles, said, 'We are going to fine you as heavily as we can' – which amounted to a total of £85. The police even expedited the departure of the four miscreants by getting British Railways to hold its Leicester train until they were ready. All this was reported under the dramatic headlines, 'JPs Blitz Youths in Skegness Prom Battle.'

The next major outbreak of trouble occurred at the Whitsun holiday. A group of about 70 youths gathered outside the Embassy dance hall – at least some of them apparently looking for trouble. Two policemen arrived and were kicked and pushed around by the mob. One of the troublemakers was identified by Chief Inspector Cranidge, who chased him through Tower Gardens. This was the signal for an outbreak of trouble and police reinforcements had to be called in – arriving just in time to pull one youth off the Chief Inspector's back. Three youths, all from Lincoln, were fined a total of £135 after this incident.

The August Bank Holiday was expected to produce further trouble, leading the Rev Laurence of Bourne to state that what the youths needed was 'rough police handling'. In fact there was little trouble that holiday, though a shortage of accommodation led to many sleeping on the beach. There were also some odd incidents – such as the way one Mod girl paid a breakfast-time visit to St Clement's parsonage: she was thrown over the six foot hedge by her 'friends'.

Easter 1965 should have seen a reopening of the troubles, but the fact that it snowed deterred many visitors on Good Friday. Trouble was restricted to an outbreak of vandalism with lavatories and other seafront buildings being damaged. However, the Mods and Rockers redressed the balance on Easter Monday, when a brawl involved over 150 youths and drove the magistrate Mr Knowles to fury. 'We are determined to stamp this thing out in Skegness,' he declared, 'this is a place where people come for pleasure and not to be annoyed.'

The disturbance began outside The Jolly Fisherman public house at closing time after lunch. The barman was trying to close up but was being pestered by youths who demanded

Some of the weapons confiscated from Mods and Rockers during the Skegness riots in the 1960s, when Bank Holiday weekends brought violence to normally peaceful seaside towns. (Lincolnshire Police Museum)

to be served. When he refused to serve any more drinks, a gang of youths began to turn the tables over and smash the bar up. The police arrived quickly and dragged a number of Lincoln youths out of the pub. One of them assaulted PC Charles but was eventually thrown into a police dog van; he kicked the van and the dog, whereupon the dog bit him. This led to a three month gaol sentence, while two others were fined £30.

While these three were safely locked up in the cells, their friends were somewhat aggrieved. A gang of 25 of them threatened to 'raid' the police station and liberate their cronies – the sort of act not seen since the 19th century. However, their nerve was not up to a full battle with the police. A fourth arrest was also made – a youth from Ilkeston was brought in for having an offensive weapon in the shape of a brick.

There were some further incidents in June 1965 that revealed unexpected sides to the Mods. A Derby youth was arrested for carrying a knife and reported that he had come to Skegness because there was going to be trouble between the 'Trogs' and the 'Thunderbirds'. 'We are Trogs,' he said, 'sort of Mods that do potholing. We are having a do at the Thunderbirds – they're a sort of Rockers.' He was fined £50 and a Nottingham youth fined £25, but the idea of a whole gang of Mods who alternated between beach brawls and potholing in the Derbyshire Peaks is a rather endearing one.

Disaster on
Somerby Hill

★

Grantham's position on the Great North Road means that it is no stranger to road traffic accidents. In the early days of motor vehicles there were a number of serious accidents on the steep hills that surround the town on every side, such as at Great Gonerby. The terrible disaster at Somerby Hill came, though, when motor cars were still in their infancy and involved a much older form of road transport – the horse-drawn cart.

George Wilkinson came from a well-established family of Kesteven farmers and tradesmen. In 1905 he was the village carrier at Lenton, about five miles south-east of Grantham. In those days the carrier was rather like a local bus company – he operated a lumbering waggon which trundled from village to village, collecting people and packages, and taking them to and from the nearest market town. It was a slow and unspectacular form of transport and would seem hardly likely to be the source of a disaster.

On 25th May 1907 George Wilkinson set out from Lenton with his waggon and a five year old mare. It was a commodious four-wheeled vehicle, capable of carrying 14 people inside in 'reasonable comfort', and another three or four on the outside. On the fateful day Wilkinson left home with his son riding 'on the step', and soon collected twelve passengers as he meandered through local hamlets. He also picked up a number of packages for the market, mostly of dairy produce.

The somnambulent ride took him through sleepy hamlets like Ingoldsby, Humby, Ropsley and Old Somerby until he emerged onto the main road at Spittlegate Heath. From there it should have been an easy journey down Somerby Hill into Grantham, though as an experienced carrier Wilkinson would have known the dangers of the hill. It was a 'double' hill, dropping sharply, levelling out, then dropping once more. As he approached the brow of the hill he became concerned about the behaviour of the horse, and decided to stop for a while before making the descent.

Witnesses were unclear as to what was the matter with the horse. One saw a 'fly' overtake and thought this could have upset it, while others tried to pin the blame on the new-fangled motor car, though none was around at the time. Wilkinson, though, had felt the horse begin to 'kick' and thought it best to calm her down before continuing; a year before she had given him 'one bit of a go' by bolting down Chapel Hill at Ropsley, and he wanted no repeat.

Wilkinson clambered out onto the roadside and went round to stand at the horse's head. According to those watching, he seemed to be having a calming effect on the horse until he slipped and fell down the side of the road. In an instant the horse bolted, taking the cart load of people off towards Somerby Hill and leaving Wilkinson lying helpless at the roadside.

As the horse bolted towards the hill the only man left in the van was labourer George Bradford from Lenton, the other passengers being all women except for Wilkinson's son. Opinions were divided as to how Bradford reacted to the situation, but some believed that he made a heroic effort to bring the horse under control. It was reported that he tried to get out to the front of the waggon to seize control of the reins, but at the vital moment he too slipped.

Poor Bradford fell out of the front of the waggon and went beneath its wheels. There was a terrible jolt as it ran over his legs and head, then it carried on its mad career. Bradford was left lying mortally injured in the road. Some saw him as a hero, but others claimed that he had really tried to escape from the waggon without being concerned about the fate of the others. The truth will never be known.

Having seen Bradford fall so horribly, the women in the

waggon began to panic. There was a door at the back and, despite the frantic pace at which the maddened horse was now galloping, Miss Florence Piggins leapt out into the road. The 47 year old housekeeper, who had been staying at Humby for a few months, hit the metalled road surface with a fearful crash and rolled over three times. She was killed instantly.

On the first part of the hill the waggon descended at speed but somehow weaved a way through the other traffic. However, when it reached the level section halfway down it veered across the road and struck the side of a waggon and two horses going from Grantham to Somerby. Ironically, this waggon was being driven by Wilkinson's brother and belonged to his father, a Somerby farmer.

The collision smashed a wheel on the carrier's waggon, causing it to crash onto one side. People, eggs and butter were flung across the road, but the horse was suddenly freed from its harness and bounded across the road. It leapt over a hedge and was later found, unharmed and apparently content, in a field nearby.

With injured people lying across the road, an urgent message was sent to Grantham for medical assistance. Four doctors arrived in a car and set about doing what they could for the injured and dying.

Bradford, aged 44, was put into a cart and taken to Grantham hospital. He died the moment he was placed onto a bed in the ward.

Among the seriously injured were 67 year old Mrs Isaacs of Ropsley, who was unconscious with haemorrhaging and 19 year old Sophia Moulds of Old Somerby, who had a fractured skull. Both were put into an omnibus accompanied by Dr Adams, but Mrs Isaacs died on her way to hospital; she had been crushed beneath the carrier's waggon when it turned over and she died from brain injuries.

Two other women, less seriously injured, were taken to the hospital in the car of the Honourable Maurice Gifford of Boothby Hall. One press report added the rather dated observation, 'All the unfortunate people belonged to the

The scene on Somerby Hill just after George Wilkinson's carrier's waggon had crashed onto its side, leaving the injured and dying flung across the road. (Lincolnshire Library Service)

working class', as if this information somehow helped to ease their sufferings.

With three people dead an inquest had to be held, though it was soon realised that in fact *two* inquests would be necessary. This bizarre situation was because Miss Piggins had died outside the Grantham borough boundary, and the other two had died inside it. It was therefore decided to hold an inquest before the Grantham borough coroner at the Guildhall on 27th July, and before the Grantham district coroner at the Spittlegate police station later the same day.

The coroner's court had to decide whether any blame could be attached to an individual. Most interest centred upon whether Wilkinson had used a horse that was known to be unsafe, but he testified that the mare was normally 'as quiet as a lamb'. He admitted that there had been a problem once before, but other witnesses supported his view that the mare was reliable.

Farmer Joel Mason, who had been behind the carrier's waggon, testified that Wilkinson had done all that he could. In Mason's opinion Wilkinson would have got the horse under control had he not fallen over at the vital moment. However, there was less agreement about the conduct of Bradford, who some thought a coward and others a hero.

An inspection had also been made of the waggon itself. The brakes were reported to be in good condition though there was a suspicion of dry rot in one of the wheels. There was no case though to suspect the waggon's condition had contributed to the accident.

The Grantham coroner's court reached a verdict of accidental death and the district coroner reached the same decision. The latter, however, observed that people who jumped out of waggons were always killed whereas those who stayed inside had a fair chance of survival. Although in 1907 there would have been many who took careful notice of his words, few would have realised that the era of the carrier's waggon was coming to an end.

Passion and Betrayal
in Alford

★

The Victorian and Edwardian period is often thought of as one of severe and uncompromising morality, but in reality this was far from the case. From King Edward VII downwards, adultery was almost as common then as it is now – but was rarely mentioned in public, certainly not among the respectable middle classes. The whole of Lincolnshire was therefore fascinated when a passionate and adulterous affair between two of Alford's 'respectable' bourgeoisie burst into the county's courts in a maelstrom of vindictive passion. Here, indeed, was a court case worthy of music hall melodrama.

That the affairs of two lovers ended in court at all was due in part to an old-fashioned belief in the value of a law which stated that a man who had promised marriage to a woman could be sued if he did not take her to the altar. So in 1907 Miss Florence Wilson of Alford brought a suit for breach of promise against Sidney Carnley, a respectable solicitor of the same town; Carnley brought a counter-suit of libel against his erstwhile lover.

Florence Wilson, born in about 1867, was the daughter of the Alford Clerk to the Justices and lived comfortably at Bleak House. Next door at Norbury House lived Sidney Carnley, an Alford lawyer with a substantial local practice and private means as well. Carnley's practice enjoyed an annual turnover of more than £3,000 whilst his private income from inherited funds allowed him to keep a stud of horses. He was among the town's leading citizens.

In 1884 Carnley married a woman of 'culture and artistic temperament' who was not, according to many witnesses, a satisfactory wife to him. In fact within a few years she had become an invalid and their characters seemed incompatible.

Carnley and Miss Wilson knew each other as neighbours, but in about 1894 the solicitor's interest in her became more than neighbourly. He told her that he had formed a liking for her and poured out the troubles of his unhappy marriage – his wife 'had never been a wife to him' and he asked Miss Wilson if she would 'give him that affection that his wife had not been able to afford'.

Miss Wilson was rather shocked by this approach and she rejected his proposition out of hand – at first. However, according to the prosecution in the later trial, Carnley 'worked his way into her affections' and they began to see each other more regularly. With the fear of scandal they had to be most circumspect, taking to hiding letters to each other in a hedge.

In the summer of 1894 Carnley promised to marry Miss Wilson as soon as he was free of his own wife. By this time Mrs Carnley was bedridden and, on occasions, Miss Wilson even helped to nurse her. Clearly, though, Florence Wilson was worried that Carnley might overstep the restrictions of the law in encouraging his wife's demise, so she (according to her own account) advised him to take better care of his wife. She also asked him to give up drinking after he was seen inebriated in public.

Carnley hid many letters in the hedge during that summer of frustrated passion, and Miss Wilson kept them all. In the first flush of excitement after asking her to marry him, Carnley wrote to Florence on 31st July 1894: 'Here I am in this most exhilarating atmosphere redeeming my promise. You see I have appropriated you. If known, the effect upon our charitable neighbours would be ghastly . . .' In his next letter, Carnley was anxious for the wedding day: 'When can I claim you for my very own before everyone?' he asked. He took to addressing Florence as 'My darling' and 'My own little one'; the latter was accurate, for Florence worried about being too small.

However, the passionate attraction between them could

not be hidden from the prying eyes of what passed for polite society in Alford. Soon the gossip had started, and Carnley was forced to allude to it in his letters to Miss Wilson. 'It is cruel that I cannot be with you, but on the contrary am tabooed . . .' Perhaps jumbling his words in the emotional stress, he said that he had become 'a social holocaust'. Opportunities to meet became limited as well: 'It is ages since I had one kiss from those dear lips that are all my own,' he complained.

Carnley gave Florence a ring as a 'representative' of their betrothal, and Miss Wilson agreed to wear it. Yet Mrs Carnley was still alive and it was difficult for them to meet – and even worse than that, they had to attend various social functions at which they pretended to have no interest in the other. 'How I should have liked to devour you this afternoon as you stood before me,' Carnley wrote, 'but what could I say or do at that time . . . simply nothing with all those eager eyes curiously prying around.'

What Carnley wanted most from Miss Wilson was the satisfaction of his carnal desires and, despite her growing attachment to him, she seems to have steadfastly held to conventional Victorian morality. During the later part of 1896 Carnley seems to have begun to look elsewhere for physical pleasure, and was seen about Alford with a 'shop girl' and even 'wicked women'.

The relationship continued despite this until, in 1900, Florence gave in to Carnley's demands and was seduced. The extent to which she was willing or unwilling in this arrangement was never really explained, but in an age when most better-off people had servants it was almost impossible to keep such things a secret. It was said that Florence often went out at about 6pm, returning home at midnight or after. In the subsequent trial the defence was happy to allege that Florence willingly went to the Carnleys' own marriage bed when Mrs Carnley was away, and brought Carnley into her own bed when she had Bleak House to herself (and a few servants).

When their respective houses were occupied things were

Norbury House, Alford, home at the turn of the century of solicitor Sidney Carnley and scene of his adulterous affair with his neighbour Florence Wilson. The house is now part of the local grammar school.

less easy, but even then they found a solution. Carnley took some rugs into his stables and they met there on about 20 occasions – according to Carnley's defence counsel. Miss Wilson denied having ever done such a thing.

The consummation of their relationship seems to have occurred in August 1900 and, according to Miss Wilson, Carnley rejected her immediately after he had achieved his wicked purposes. 'Now you can tell Alford what you are,' he told her ungallantly, though most of Alford seems to have had a suspicion already. When he saw her in the street he started to cross over to avoid her.

Almost inevitably in such a melodramatic tale, Miss Wilson found that she was pregnant. She followed convention by immediately leaving the town and went to live in Southwell for a while, where she was attended by Dr Herbert. There were later allegations that Dr Herbert attended to her in ways that were more than just professional, but this may have been a ruse by Carnley's side to blacken Miss Wilson's name.

After she went off to Wimbledon to have the baby, Herbert seems to have acted as a go-between for her and Carnley. He arranged that the solicitor should send her £90 for expenses although Carnley extracted a promise in return that he should not be troubled on the matter again. The child was duly born, but died within a week. Miss Wilson later claimed that she returned all the money to Carnley.

With no child to hide she was safe to return to Alford, and Carnley declared that he still loved her. Miss Wilson, though, found that her enthusiasms were now tempered by experience and she told the ardent solicitor that 'one tragedy is enough'. By March 1902 she seems to have changed her mind and wrote to Carnley asking when she could meet him again. She was worried that other 'wicked women' were now involved with him, though Carnley had his suspicions that Miss Wilson was worried about her long-term financial position.

Miss Wilson began to take unpleasant steps to further her ambitions and to gratify her anger. She wrote to Carnley, telling him 'I shall expose you so that the populace will laugh at you, and you can go home and cry to your wife, and whine like a puppy.' Mrs Carnley also received poison pen letters, undoubtedly from Wilson, which bluntly asked, 'Why don't you poison yourself, you old hag?'

In January 1906 Mrs Carnley died but Carnley failed to show the expected interest in finally marrying his paramour. In fact he positively refused to, even when Dr Herbert wrote to him suggesting that it was a good time to settle things properly. Carnley felt that in April 1901 they had agreed together that the 'engagement' should be called off and that he therefore had no further responsibility in the matter.

Florence Wilson then became the furious woman scorned of legend. In October 1906 she wrote to Carnley demanding that he marry her 'or I shall expose you as a dishonourable man'. She began to follow him around the town and arranged to have photographs taken of him with other women, which she had printed off as postcards with various insulting messages attached. Other messages, some of them obscene, were chalked up on the doors and walls of his house, including 'You are a creature known as ''would but can't''.' There were also comments to the effect that Carnley was a good judge of horses for breeding, but could not ride himself.

This outpouring of bile shocked and amused the citizens of Alford, but when Miss Wilson decided to sue for breach of promise the case came to the attention of the whole of the county. There was a complex legal preamble, when Carnley's defence tried to argue that a promise of marriage made while a man was still married was not a legal promise. When the case reached trial in Lincoln, Wilson sued for breach of promise while Carnley counter-sued over the publication of libellous postcards. The jury decided that both claims were true; they awarded Florence Wilson £100 damages for having been jilted, and they awarded Carnley an insulting one farthing's damages for having been libelled. The mysterious Dr Herbert was not there to see the close – he had to go home to have a poisoned finger amputated.

The First Plane
to Lincoln

★

The summer of 1912 can probably be described as 'the summer of the aeroplane' as far as Lincolnshire was concerned, for it saw the first flights by powered aircraft into and around the county. These flights excited huge interest and massive crowds gathered to see the first machines – encouraged by the *Daily Mail*, which organised several of the flights as a promotional venture.

The honour of being the first aviator to land in Lincoln must go to a Scot, Mr W Ewen, though he did not accomplish his feat without great difficulty in his 60hp French-built Caudron. Sponsored by the *Daily Mail*, he was making a tour along the east coast and was due to fly from Peterborough to Lincoln on 7th July 1912. It was arranged that he would leave the Peterborough 'airfield' at Walton at about 10am and land at the Stamp End Athletic Club's ground in Wragby Road, Lincoln. Although the crowds waited patiently for his arrival, all hope of a flight on 7th July was prevented by strong winds.

Ewen's flight was postponed until the next day and he made two attempts to set off from Walton that morning. Both had to be aborted due to a misfiring engine and a stiff breeze.

At 5.55pm he finally left Walton and the news was soon telegraphed to Lincoln. Huge crowds again began to gather at all the best vantage points, such as Lindum Hill, and there were about 15,000 people at the grammar school which was adjacent to the athletic ground. It had been arranged that Ewen would land at the athletic ground and many people paid the 6d entrance fee to be sure of the best view – a mistake, as it turned out!

At 6.30pm news came through that Ewen's plane had been seen flying over Bourne, following the railway line northwards to Sleaford. He was 'flying beautifully' it was reported. Excitement built up in Lincoln, but half an hour later there had been no more news. By 7.30pm people began to fear that Ewen must have crashed and then another telegram arrived with the terse message 'Down at Scopwick'. Did this mean disaster?

In fact there had not been a disaster – Ewen had lost his way. He had passed 500 ft over Ruskington at about 6.40pm but gathering clouds had begun to make navigation difficult, so after Digby he began to descend over the Lincoln road. He put down in a field at Sheffield House, Scopwick, to ask directions.

As can be imagined, the arrival of the aircraft caused a sensation in the village. Quiet, unassuming Scopwick was to go down in history as the landing point for the first aircraft in Lincolnshire. Locals turned out in force, which was just as well, for Ewen needed half a dozen strong men to help him get the plane ready for take-off again.

Gustave Hamel's aircraft, photographed near Grimsby in July 1912. Hamel became the first man to fly across the Humber after W. Ewen's attempt was prevented by bad weather. (Welholme Galleries, Grimsby)

71

Although the light was beginning to fade, Ewen decided to press on to Lincoln and at about 8.45pm was airborne again. In Lincoln people had begun to despair of his arrival, and as the cathedral clock struck nine o'clock many began to drift homewards. Their progress was halted by a sudden cry of 'He's coming!'

The grammar school clock stood at 9.04pm as Ewen's aircraft passed overhead, a sight that produced paroxysms of delight in all the journalists watching. According to one, everyone had 'a view of his machine in flight that was nothing short of magnificent . . . there was something weird about the sight as well as grandeur.'

Ewen made a circuitous approach to the landing ground, flying out over the prison to Greetwell and Reepham before turning back along Wragby Road. Signal rockets were fired to guide him to the landing strip, but at this point the lateness of the hour – and possibly his rashness in continuing from Scopwick – almost proved Ewen's undoing. In the gloom he underestimated his distance from the athletic ground and came down instead in a field of barley. According to those watching, the plane's propeller got entangled in the crop, causing it to flip over and come to a halt just before a wire fence. Ewen later said that he deliberately crashed the plane because he was afraid of going through the fence into a crowd of spectators.

When the plane 'turned turtle', many in the crowd were horrified and there were gasps of terror. Some rushed over to the plane and there were cheers of delight when Ewen was seen to struggle to his feet, slightly dazed but none the worse for his accident. One of the most bizarre ceremonies in Lincolnshire's history then occurred: Chief Constable Crawley led three cheers for Ewen and then he was greeted officially by the Mayor and Sheriff of Lincoln. With all the dignitaries standing waist deep in the barley, the Mayor presented Ewen with a diamond-studded Imp tie-pin. He was then taken off to The Saracen's Head to recuperate.

Ewen's flight actually helped to cause a bizarre motor accident on the road between Branston and Lincoln. Several cars had been trying to follow the plane on the ground, the occupants standing up in their seats and swaying dangerously whilst the speeding convoy threw up a huge cloud of dust from the road. Near the top of Canwick Hill the cavalcade crossed the path of a farmer from Bracebridge Heath, who was going to Lincoln with his motorbike and a cart attached, and a boy cycling to Branston. It all ended with the boy catapulted into a ditch but although he was knocked out, no injuries were sustained.

Ewen had to get a new propeller for his plane and repairs to the aircraft itself were made by Gilbert & Son of Melville Street. Whilst recovering, Ewen announced that he would be doing test flights from West Common but requested that the crowd should be kept under better control. He said that unless the onlookers kept away from the aircraft he would be forced to leave Lincoln without further flights.

In the event he decided not to do any 'demonstration flights', but planned to leave from West Common on 12th July. He intended to fly to Hull by way of Riseholme, Hackthorn, Normanby, Waddingham, Brigg and Barton. Newsagents in the area sold postcards for despatch by 'aerial post' – Ewen would take them by plane to Hull, where they would be specially stamped, then put into the normal mail. A great crowd gathered at the West Common to watch his departure which was scheduled for 6pm. However, just as the plane was being prepared there was a terrific thunderstorm. The mechanic, Mr Warren, grabbed a police horse's cape and threw it over the plane's engine but the severe winds caused damage to the struts and wires.

It was fortunate that the storm did not come later and catch Ewen in flight. It caused a lot of damage in Lincolnshire, killing some animals at Nettleham and causing the Middle Rasen carrier's cart to crash after the horse got an electric shock and bolted, tipping the passengers across the road and into a ditch.

Ewen tried again the following day but the weather was still poor. He decided to abandon the idea of flying to Hull and had Gilbert & Son take the plane to pieces for sending by land. The people of Lincoln were bitterly disappointed.

Ewen's failure meant that the first flight across the Humber was achieved by Gustave Hamel on 16th July. Travelling from Hull to Grimsby, he took 16 minutes and flew at 2,000ft to avoid the sea mists. He spent two triumphant days in Grimsby.

The promoters of the Lincolnshire show, which was held at Skegness in 1912, decided to take advantage of the craze for aircraft by hiring Mr J Brereton to appear with his Blackburn Monoplane. He made the first flight there on 18th July, cruising over the Vine Hotel and the beach. Skegness was later used to film some of the flight scenes for the film, *Those Magnificent Men in Their Flying Machines*.

Lincoln's summer of aircraft was not quite over. At the end of the month, a Mr Hucks brought another plane to Lincoln and made a number of exhibition flights from West Common including one daredevil passage between the towers of the cathedral. Thus the Air Age began in Lincoln, but it was soon to turn from fun to the utmost seriousness – for Ruston's began to make aircraft for use during the Great War.

The Great Flood
of 1953

★

When the corner shops of Lincolnshire received their copies
of the *Echo* on 31st January 1953, they found that it reported
'Gales Lash Lincs – 63mph gust.' The maximum wind
speed was recorded at RAF Cranwell, but the chief news
story was about a major disaster in the Irish Sea with the loss
of the ferry, *Princess Victoria*. The weather forecast predicted
that it would be, 'Squally. An intense depression off NE
Scotland will move SE . . . chance of severe gales in places.
Bright periods, some squally showers. Cold.'

This grim weather forecast led to one of the blackest days
in the history of Lincolnshire, for 31st January 1953 was the
day of the catastrophic East Coast floods that devastated the
coast of England from the Tyne to the Thames. A total of 41
lives were lost in Lincolnshire and the area around
Mablethorpe and Sutton-on-Sea was almost totally wrecked
by the flood waters.

The cause of the disaster was a particular combination of
weather conditions that had been dreaded by meteorologists
and flood defence engineers. An atmospheric depression
moved south-eastwards over the North Sea; this lightening
of air pressure allowed the sea-level to rise above its normal
tidal position and the waves were further whipped up by the
presence of an anticyclone to the west, causing high winds.
The winds produced waves of up to 20 ft high and the
combination of weather conditions resulted in a high tide
about eight ft above normal levels and one that was
considerably prolonged by the 'surge tide' caused by the
depression.

The effects were felt all along the Lincolnshire coast – the

75

seawater began to surmount the defences at Sutton as the river Witham at Boston began to flood, hemmed in by the high tides in the Wash. The Mablethorpe coastguard phoned a warning to the authorities – 'The waves are smashing the sea wall to hell. Bad flooding is certain.'

At 5.25pm the sea defences collapsed at Sandilands and the sea forced a gap in the dunes at Acre Gap. Between Mablethorpe and Ingoldmells the sea forced ten breaches in the defences and wrecked the promenades at both Mablethorpe and Ingoldmells. Some 860,000 tons of sand were washed into Mablethorpe while in Sutton some of the streets were eight ft deep in sand.

Cars floated down Sutton High Street and the Beach Hotel was flooded very quickly at 5.30pm. Sisters Valerie and Jillian Blair were trapped inside the wrecked building for eight hours, clinging to the remains of the second floor as furniture floated away. The tide should have gone down at 6.30pm, but it remained very high until midnight when they were able to wade to safety at the Bacchus Hotel. Six bodies were found in a garage at Sutton.

As the water flooded across the flat coastal marshes, there were dramatic scenes and tragic incidents. In Mablethorpe PC Midgley helped to rescue 16 people, accommodating most of them in his own house. He leapt from an upstairs window to rescue an elderly couple in the water and also saved a 14 year old paper boy. The Lynne family escaped to safety by commandeering a railway plate-layer's trolley.

At Saltfleet the sea breached the defences in Sea Lane. Four people drowned in nearby bungalows, all of them elderly. At Suggitt's Bay the sea broke through the railway embankment and flooded 1,000 houses. There were major breaches of the defences at Sea Bank Farm, Elder Cottage and Chapel Six Marshes; the sea also swept away one of the natural defences – sand dunes, 300 yards of which were flattened at Sutton. Once the sea had penetrated these outlying bastions, it flooded over the flat land between them and the Roman Bank. In the areas between, such as Chapel Marsh, there was little chance of houses escaping the

A coastal chalet left perched precariously after the flood waters had receded. Sea defences all along the Lincolnshire coast proved no match for the combination of tides and fierce winds in early 1953.

devastating effects of the flood.

Much of Ingoldmells was built in this gap between the Roman Bank and the sea wall. Six feet of water inundated the area, and there were 17 deaths in the area as the sea swept a mile inland. Many people were trapped inside their houses as the waters rose inexorably; Rev Walter Last and his wife struggled to force an escape through the ceiling of their bungalow but drowned as they tried. Almost the same thing happened in the house of the Chambers family, where Bill Chambers and five of his family were drowned. In Mablethorpe, Mrs June Laurence was lucky to have an upstairs to drag her children to. One mother in the town lost her grip on her baby and saw it swept away.

Further south, Butlin's at Skegness was between three and six feet under water but the winter season saved it from being the scene of disaster. The town of Skegness was also saved by its own natural defences − it had a very wide foreshore and promenade, dissipating the strength of the flood. Despite this, the sea had surrounded the clock tower by 8pm and the Tower Cinema had to be evacuated; the sea advanced halfway up Lumley Road and the gardens were ruined. The most ironic event in Skegness was that three former lifeboats were in the Princes Parade car park being prepared for the summer season – and were washed out to sea. However, a hundred boats from the Skegness boating lake were later taken to Ingoldmells where they helped rescue many people, including 13 who had forced their way through a ceiling but had been trapped in a false roof.

To the north of the stricken area, RAF North Coates had to be evacuated while at Cleethorpes the bathing pool was filled with sand, and the area between the pier and Wonderland was wrecked. Further north, there were many minor breaches of the defences between Grimsby and Killingholme; in Grimsby, a thousand people were made temporarily homeless. A ship was turned on its side in Immingham dry dock, while a lightship capsized. The power station and three factories had to be closed. In the extreme south of the region, 70 houses at Sutton Bridge were flooded by the Nene and 110 acres were flooded at Gedney Marsh. At Spalding the Welland flooded a dozen houses and a pub.

Further inland across Lincolnshire, gales and rain caused devastation though not to the same degree. A Gainsborough WVS worker collapsed and died in a car while delivering blankets, and the stalls at Horncastle market were wrecked.

With daylight on 1st February rescuers hurried into the area, and reporters too. Many were gripped by the urgency of the task, for marooned survivors had to be rescued before further high tides swept them away. One reporter described the scene at Mablethorpe that evening:

'As mountainous waves, still lashed by gale force winds, began to crash against the wrecked sea defences at Mablethorpe and Trusthorpe last night, a shuttle service of hundreds of lorries, buses, boats and an amphibian continued the race against the tide to evacuate the last remaining people . . .'

The Duke of Edinburgh was amongst those who came to see the flood devastation for themselves and to give what comfort they could.

Another journalist visited Mablethorpe earlier that afternoon and saw crowds of refugees: 'What a pitiful scene it was, and how unreal it seemed on a bright Sunday afternoon.' He plucked up a postcard of sunny Mablethorpe as it floated by.

At 9am on 2nd February it was announced that the entire Mablethorpe and Sutton area would have to be evacuated. There was a danger of disease, but the authorities were also worried about looting and the possibility of renewed flooding with the next high tide. The people of the area were moved to Louth and Alford, it being decided that the area should remain closed for three weeks. A special medical team was sent from Nocton RAF hospital and they set up a base at Alford school. Many slept in Alford town hall while a cafe in the town gave 300 breakfasts; 2,000 people were accommodated in Louth. Inquests on the dead were held at Louth Infirmary, but on 3rd February there was still no real idea as to how many dead there were. There were reports of 'hundreds' missing and descriptions of floating bodies at Mablethorpe and Sutton.

79

By the early afternoon of 2nd February the water level in Mablethorpe had fallen to 18 inches, but even so there were still 200 people who refused to be evacuated. At Sutton the waters were still four feet deep. It was estimated at this stage that there were 6,000 homeless and over 15,000 acres flooded. The area was also still dangerous – four pressmen narrowly escaped death when caught by high waves on the sea wall between Sutton and Mablethorpe. Harold Macmillan, then the Minister for Housing, toured the area in an amphibious vehicle.

The scale of the damage was enormous. Thirty four miles of sea defences had been ruined and 4,000 men were needed to help in repairs. In the rush to plug the defences before further flooding, 25,000 tons a day were added to the sea wall. The huge breach at Acre Gap was filled using 40,000 tons of slag, which was brought by train from Scunthorpe. The Army was called in to try and plug the gap at Trusthorpe and a temporary wall was quickly put up between Church Lane, Mablethorpe and Sandilands.

A 28 year old soldier was arrested for looting cigarettes and cutlery at Mablethorpe. He was given six months in gaol. The more helpful efforts of his colleagues continued to be needed as further gale warnings were issued on 4th February; the temporary wall was breached and further flooding caused and the sea flowed through the streets of Mablethorpe once more.

The battle against Nature continued for days. On 12th February, amidst snow and sleet, further flooding was expected at Mablethorpe and Sutton, where a BBC reporter described men struggling to build the defences in 'fiendish conditions, bitterly cold and wind driving the snow.'

This battle was eventually won, but the on-going war against the sea will never be won. To this day the engineers continue to repair, reinforce and redesign the sea defences in the certain knowledge that no system will ever be totally secure. The lesson of 1953 was that too many people were allowed to live close to the sea without adequate protection; what can seem a pretty scene in the summer, can be a murderous beast in the winter gales.

Binbrook's
Carpet King

★

A heartwarming rags-to-riches story that reflected well on the charitable people of Lincolnshire appeared in the national newspapers during the summer of 1937. The occasion was the return to England of an American celebrity millionaire, Harutune Michaelyan, who had been set on his road to fortune by the kind people of Binbrook. Michaelyan, who was staying in a suite at the Savoy Hotel in London, repaid a debt of gratitude by returning to spend a few days in the more humble homes of the village that had fostered him.

Michaelyan was an Armenian whose parents had been victims of massacre by the Turks in about 1900. With a number of other orphaned children he was brought to England as, he later put it, 'a little waif'. Once in Britain there were few homes and no work available for the young Armenians, but their plight must have got into the newspapers for a Binbrook shoemaker, Mr Fridlington, heard all about it. He wrote to the authorities, stating simply that 'I would like to take one of these Armenian boys and learn him shoemaking.'

Young Michaelyan was selected and wrote back to Mr Fridlington. The kind shoemaker sent him another letter, telling him to get the train to Louth from where a carrier's cart would take him over the Wolds to Binbrook. However, something went wrong, for Michaelyan got the train to Market Rasen instead – from where there was no carrier's cart to Binbrook on that day. It was pouring with rain, but he managed to walk the eight miles along unknown lanes to his new home. The millionaire later described this stage of his travels as 'a terribly long walk in a strange country'.

When he got to Binbrook he saw a 'Fridlington' sign near the market and knocked at the door. At first Mrs Fridlington mistook him for someone else. 'Hello, Moses,' were her words of greeting to him. The Armenian boy soon became a sensation as news of his arrival spread around Binbrook – no-one as exotic as an Armenian had ever been seen there before. His presence attracted such interest that parents would hold up their small children at the Fridlingtons' windows so they could get a look at him.

Mr Fridlington taught Michaelyan the basic skills of shoemaking but died soon afterwards and the business was sold to Mr E Briggs – with whom Michaelyan came back to stay years later. The young Armenian decided that he could not hope to make his fortune in Binbrook and resolved to go to London, but the villagers did not see this as a rejection of their hospitality – indeed they collected three guineas to speed him on his way, and Michaelyan kept a note of the names of all those who gave donations.

He was very popular in Binbrook and many were sad to see him go. 'Now Harutune, be careful,' were the last words spoken to him as he left. Years afterwards the millionaire was able to look back on this advice with amusement: 'They had a very lively fear of the pitfalls which might beset a young man in London, had the village people of the day.'

In London Michaelyan gave up his shoemaking trade and began to deal in Eastern embroideries using knowledge he had brought with him from Armenia. Over four years he managed to build up savings of £700 and decided to use this to go to America, which he saw as the land of real opportunity. It is a sign of the close ties he had with Binbrook that when he sailed from Liverpool it was a Binbrook man, Alfred Whitworth, who stood on the quay and waved him off.

In New York Michaelyan made one of the most important mistakes of his life. He decided to invest his capital in a real estate project, but this was something he knew nothing about. He lost everything, and resolved to always concentrate on trade where he had an expert knowledge.

He began to build up a new business in Eastern carpets

and soon opened a shop on Madison Avenue; eventually his emporium was described as 'a great gallery'. He began to import the finest Persian carpets and rugs to sell to the rich of New York, but he always kept the best examples for his own personal collection. With success came more shops, including one in Palm Beach. By the time Michaelyan returned to Britain in 1937 he was famous as the 'Carpet King', the world authority on rugs and carpets for the glittering set, selling them for 'princely sums'.

Yet Michaelyan never forgot the people who had set him on the road to fortune and, on his triumphal return, decided to pay them a visit. 'Binbrook,' he said, 'is still one of the finest places in the world to me, and I made as many friends here as I have made in many years elsewhere.'

The Birth of
the Tank

★

In 1916, headlines in national newspapers told of a new weapon being unleashed by British troops on the Western Front – the tank. Lincoln was the birthplace of the tank – the special land weapon that was born out of the frustration and slaughter of trench deadlock that characterised much of the First World War.

When war broke out in August 1914 many of the top generals believed that it would be an 'open' war in which the lightning charges of the cavalry would be the most important force. They were proved dismally wrong – the horse continued to be used for transport, but as a weapon of assault it was all but useless in the mud of Flanders and Picardy. The conditions in the battlefields resembled a ploughed field more than anything else and so it was perhaps natural that military problems attracted the attention of Lincolnshire engineering firms, who mainly catered for an agricultural trade.

One of the firms involved was William Foster & Co of Lincoln. They had started out in 1854 as flour millers but in 1856 opened the Wellington foundry and moved into engineering. At the start of the war in 1914 they were employing 350 men but this rapidly expanded to 2,000 as they gained military contracts.

The managing director of Foster's was William Tritton. At the start of the war he became involved in advising on how to move heavy howitzers across boggy ground. The result was a design for a 105hp tractor which had wheels, not a caterpillar track, and was equipped with a portable bridge. A subsequent design was a tractor with an eight ft portable bridge but this proved too heavy for the Flanders conditions. The solution to moving heavy machinery over muddy ground was, of course, the endless chain track or 'caterpillar' track. This had been first developed successfully by Hornsby's of Grantham under the direction of their works manager, David Roberts. Although demonstrations were made to the military about six years before the start of the war, Hornsby's sold only one machine based on the caterpillar system – built in association with Foster's. Hornsby's sold the rights to the invention to an American company for £4,000 – another example of how British industrial opportunity was lost through lack of vision and management, rather than through failure of technical expertise.

The idea of building an armoured vehicle to break through the enemy defences was suggested by Colonel Ernest Swinton in October 1914, but aroused little interest in the Army. It was Winston Churchill, at the Admiralty, who was first captivated by the idea and he set up a committee to pursue it. The project was planned by a Lincolnshire man, Sir Tennyson d'Eyncourt, the Director of Naval Construction. On 30th July 1915 Tritton was asked to work with Major W Wilson on the designs for a 'landship'. It was agreed that this should use American 'Bullock' caterpillar tracks but it needed to have a life of only 50 miles – in the context of the Western Front, this was an enormous distance.

The first tank, named *Little Willie*, was designed and built at Foster's within the space of 37 days. It made its first trial run on 14th September 1915 but on a further trial lost its tracks. Tritton made some improvements to their design and *Little Willie* was tested with new tracks in Burton Park on 3rd December. However, it failed to meet the requirements of Colonel Swinton.

As a result, it was decided to build a bigger tank with a forward nose. The new tank was completed on 6th January 1916 and named *Big Willie*, though it was also known as *Mother*. It was first tested in a field near the Tritton works on 14th January and then taken to Burton Park at night on 19th January to test its guns. On the night of 27th January *Mother*

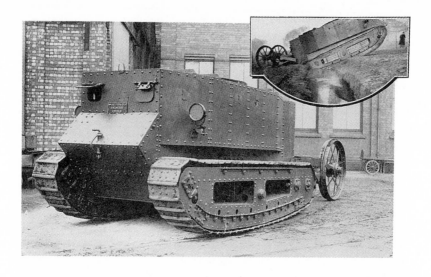

Little Willie (top) was the first tank to be designed and built by William Foster & Co of Lincoln in 1915, Big Willie (or Mother) (below) following soon after. William Tritton, managing director of Foster's, came to be credited with the invention of the tank, a response to the terrible battlefield conditions faced by the troops at the Front. (Lincolnshire Library Service)

left by train for Hatfield where it had several days of testing. On 2nd February it was demonstrated to top politicians like Balfour and Lloyd-George and top army officers like Kitchener. On 8th February King George watched a demonstration as well.

The reception was not altogether favourable, though this was perhaps unsurprising as the British general staff in the Great War seem to have been unified by a lack of vision, imagination and intelligence. Kitchener scorned the tank as 'a pretty mechanised toy'.

The result was that Foster's were contracted to build 25 tanks, though this was soon increased to 150. Other firms were brought in to help with the order, while the completed tanks were sent to Elvedon in Norfolk. The first mock battle was fought there on 6th October. The whole project was given the highest level of secrecy and the new machines got their name of 'tanks' as rumours were spread that they were mobile water tanks for use on the Russian front or in Mesopotamia – some even had Russian letters painted on the sides.

The tanks first saw action on 15th September 1916 and on 22nd September Tritton was able to watch their use in an attack on Thiepval. There was some disagreement in the Army over their initial use and the tanks were pressed into service too quickly, meaning that their surprise value was lost at a time when only a few were available for battle. This was largely the fault of the blundering General Haig, who wanted to redeem his Somme offensive and cared little for longer term issues.

Tritton was also involved in the construction of the *Whippet* type of tank, which could travel at 9mph rather than 2.5mph. Four hundred of these were ordered in 1917 and the Foster's works was turned over to constructing them. Part of the Boultham estate was purchased for a test ground. The Midland Railway laid in a special siding for the increased tank traffic. Another type to be designed was the *Hornet*, but the war ended before these were ever used in battle.

The story of Tritton's contribution to the Great War may

seem to be a simple one of engineering genius, but life is never straightforward. After the war a furious row broke out over rival claims to have invented the tank. Rear Admiral Sir Murray Sueter claimed that it was he who had come up with the crucial idea of using caterpillar tracks; he argued that at the Admiralty landship meeting on 4th March 1915 Tritton's design had been a ridiculous 'tractor engine on wheels with a kind of armoured shield in front of the driver.' It was also claimed that 'an armoured car officer' had persuaded Tritton of the value of caterpillar tracks while Major Wilson, the man who had worked with Tritton, pressed his own case.

The Government set up a committee to investigate the various claims to have invented the tank. The Royal Commisson on Awards to Inventors sat in October 1919 and decided to credit the invention jointly to Tritton and Major Wilson, each receiving £15,000. There were complaints that Tritton had already been 'adequately rewarded' through the profits made by his company. The controversy did not die there, for in 1925 an action was brought against the Government for compensation. The fairest assessment would seem to be that it was Swinton who first conceived of the tank as it came to be built and who first considered how it might be best used in battle; it was Wilson and Tritton who translated his ideas into something of steel. Swinton, though, had many enemies on the General Staff and was denied the credit that he was due – as indeed was Tennyson d'Eyncourt, another to be pushed aside when his ideas conflicted with the orthodoxies of the day.

Death at the
Crossing

★

Most towns are visited by tragedy occasionally and at such times friends and neighbours cluster around to give support to the bereaved. It is unusual, though, for tragedy to strike down several people from one street in an instance, but just such a thing happened in the Lincoln crossing tragedy of 1922. As a result, one of the largest funerals ever to take place in the city was held around the tiny Boultham chapel.

Four young men from the Lincoln suburb of Boultham went out for an evening's ratting on 11th May 1922. They were all from a labouring background, living in the working class district of Beresford Street. The group included Thomas Pyrah, 25, and his brother-in-law, Fred Wheatley, 23, who both lived at no 34. Pyrah had been an assistant Scoutmaster for a number of years. With them was Leonard Abell, 19, from no 14, who also had connections with the Scouts. Last of the group was Arthur Briggs, aged 17, from no 31. That they came from fairly poor backgrounds was shown by a lack of photographs of them – no picture had been taken of Abell or Briggs since they were at junior school.

At about 10.30pm the group of young men were returning from their ratting trip and came to the Coulson Road railway crossing. This was an accommodation crossing for pedestrians only and was protected only by a latch gate, not by any signal or railwaymen.

A goods train was leaving Lincoln St Mark's station on its way towards Nottingham, passing along the further of the two tracks as the men approached the crossing. Giving a cursory look along the other track towards Nottingham, they stepped out onto the line to watch the goods train go by.

In the 1920s all trains carried oil lamps so as to be seen in the dark, but the lamps were not always effective. None of the young men saw the approach of the 9pm passenger train from Nottingham, which was running late and due into Lincoln at 10.12pm. Its driver, Samuel Sutton, later swore that he had checked the lamps at Collingham and they were working satisfactorily. When he arrived at Lincoln he found the lamp out.

What had happened was simple but terrible. The young men had not noticed the approach of the passenger train as its lamp was out, nor had they heard it due to the clanking passage of the goods. Foolishly, they had stepped out onto the Lincoln track and been either mown down by the passenger train or caught between it and the goods.

The first that was known of the tragic death of four young men was discovered by Ben Harwin. He came across the crossing shortly after the accident and noticed a strange shape at the lineside. He struck a match to get a better view and found, to his horror, that the shape was a body.

The police were called and it was only then that the full extent of the disaster began to emerge. PC Stevenson inspected the body at the crossing, which was that of Briggs. A search along the track towards Lincoln uncovered the corpse of Abell 25 yards away, lying between the two tracks. Forty eight yards further along, Pyrah was dead between the rails of the Lincoln line and another 250 yards away was Wheatley, who had been carried almost as far as the Boultham crossing.

The news was communicated to the Midland station, where Sutton inspected his engine and found it covered in blood. However, neither Sutton nor his fireman had noticed anything of particular significance at the crossing. A police surgeon, Dr Coleman, arrived on the scene at 10.50pm and checked the cause of death of the victims. Of course there was no doubt about this, but Coleman was appalled at the terrible injuries they had received to the head – three of them had been almost decapitated.

The funeral on 15th May was a sad day for Lincoln. In

The funeral of the four young men killed at the Coulson Road railway crossing in Lincoln in May 1922 was one of the largest to ever take place in the city. (Lincolnshire Library Service)

Beresford Street every blind was down and every curtain drawn in respect, and a whole area of Lincoln virtually closed down for the time of the funeral. Thousands lined the streets between the homes of the victims and the Boultham Park cemetery.

The procession was accompanied by 150 Scouts in honour of Pyrah and Abell, while 100 workmen from Foster's and Ruston's also accompanied the cortège. The coffins of Pyrah and Abell were covered with Union Jacks in honour of their war service.

The tiny church in the cemetery was reserved for the families of the deceased, except for one pew where the Mayor and the old Boultham school headteacher sat. Hundreds of mourners watched from in the churchyard and from outside its railings. They were able to join in the singing as a harmonium was placed in the cemetery and played by the current Boultham headteacher. The Last Post was sounded at the graveside by a Scout. All four young men were buried side by side.

Some steps were taken to help the bereaved families. A collection and fund was organised and this was able to give out £15 to help them over the first few days. A number of charitable efforts were made in the city, with concerts by the Malleable Ironworks brass band and the Salvation Army.

Summer of Discontent

★

The years before the First World War were a troubled time in industrial relations. Over the previous decades the unions had gradually eroded the legal restrictions that had weakened their capacity to campaign on behalf of their members, while the employers had responded to this by forming themselves into employers' associations. In Lincolnshire this process especially affected the heavy industrial works in Lincoln and Gainsborough.

Firms like Clayton & Shuttleworth, Ruston's and Robey's were experiencing long-running problems with their workers. Leading the dispute was the Boilermakers' Society, which had declared a ban on overtime from 6th November 1910. The dispute was over pay and conditions; wages at the time were 33s per week for a riveter, 35s for a plater and 37s for an angle-smith.

This dispute dragged on for months with both sides adopting tactics to put pressure on the other. The employers did all they could to encourage men to break the overtime ban, causing resentment among those who had sacrificed their additional earnings. Eventually tempers built up until the first case hit the headlines.

William Clayton came before Lincoln magistrates on 25th July 1911 to allege that he had been assaulted by six men who worked for Ruston, Proctor & Co. In the hearing the prosecution alleged that these six were 'intelligent working men' who 'could not control their passions and evil tempers.'

Clayton was an experienced workman who had spent 17 years with Robey's and over two years at Ruston's. For a time he had been a member of the Machine Workers' Association but on 1st November 1910 had begun to pay subscriptions to the Gasworkers' Union, which was in alliance with the Boilermakers'. Much of the bitterness of the case surrounded Clayton's union membership, since he claimed he was not a union member while the defence claimed that he was – though he had failed to pay his full subscription.

Clayton had been one of the men who worked extra time at Ruston's, for which he was followed home by the other men and called 'blackleg' or 'traitor'. The crowd who waited for him and other breakers of the union code was often over 500 strong, so Ruston's varied their working hours and provided taxis home to beat the pickets. However, on 20th July Clayton left the works at 5pm to find a large and angry crowd waiting for him. He decided to run.

His first idea was to run through Cannon's glue works, but the mob caught up with him and threw him into the river Witham at its worst place – just where the effluent of the glue works was discharged, untreated, into its murky waters. At least Clayton got some revenge out of his ducking, for he dragged one of his assailants in with him. After the ducking he was allowed to go home 'in the most stinking condition . . . with a large quantity of beastly stuff on him.'

During the hearing before the magistrates, Clayton was heckled with shouts of 'Which way are you leaving?' There were allegations that Ruston's had encouraged him to bring the prosecution and were paying his costs. The six defendants were found guilty and sentenced to a fine of 30s or two weeks in prison.

By this time there were already signs that the bad feeling between worker and employer was going to spread. On 23rd July the Amalgamated Society of Railway Servants staged a demonstration in Boston, led by the Kirton Brass Band and starring a dog with a collecting box.

On 26th July the Boilermakers' Society declared a strike, and 1,000 Lincoln men downed their tools and walked out. On the same day the Gainsborough firm of Marshall, Sons & Co locked out 100 of its own boilermakers – and so the

Dunn & Sons' broken window was part of the damage caused by the increasingly violent industrial disputes and strikes that took place in Lincoln in 1911. (Lincoln Library Local Studies Collection)

battle lines were drawn. Feelings between strikers and 'blacklegs' soon ran high – in early August there was trouble in Lincoln High Street and a mob attacked a man at Cornhill. In Gainsborough Marshall's replied to the pickets by providing beds and meals within the factory for those who had accepted their conditions.

It was against this background of gathering tension that a new and national factor caused the outbreak of real violence in Lincoln. On Friday 18th August, the Amalgamated Society of Railway Servants declared the first national railway strike, winning the sympathy of many of Lincoln's young men. At the Midland railway station 50 men went on strike out of 106 staff, whilst the Great Central was virtually paralysed by the loss of 40 men from Central station. There was a rumour that a GCR train from Grimsby to Lincoln was stranded at Reepham after its driver made a sudden decision to join the strike. A few trains continued to run and rumours spread rapidly that an attempt was to be made to block the famous level crossings in the High Street in order to prevent their passage.

By 9.30pm a crowd several thousand strong had gathered at the crossing outside Central station, and had successfully prevented two 'blackleg' trains from leaving. Chief Constable Coleman arrived with a force of officers and led a baton charge to clear the crossing. The police succeeded in their aim, with the price being an injury to PC Capes' head. With the crossing cleared, the signalman – an elderly man enduring 'an anxious and precarious vigil' within a stone's throw of the crowd – signalled the two trains through. Both were greeted with boos and more missiles. The *Lincolnshire Chronicle* felt that genuine strikers were not involved. The driver of a train from Grantham was stoned at Canwick bridge.

The problems of the Friday night were only a faint warning of what was to follow. During Saturday the police guarded the level crossings and the railways attempted to run a service – with the Central stationmaster helping out on gate duty. Expecting significant trouble, the police camped at a secret location in New Boultham where they expected an attack on the signalbox. The important Durham Ox crossing was also guarded.

By 11.20pm a large crowd had gathered in the High Street despite there being 80 police at the High Bridge. When the police drew their batons the crowd dispersed, but only to wreck and smash in many other places throughout the city. The Great Eastern Railway's office in St Mark's Square was attacked, Bass & Co's office at the Midland station set on fire and the GCR signalbox at Pelham Street Junction wrecked. Its bell was stolen and rung in the streets. Widespread looting of shops in the High Street took place, with many stolen items simply being thrown into the river. Several policemen barricaded themselves into the Queen's Hotel and telephoned for outside help, while most windows in High Street were broken.

Extra police and soldiers had already been summoned. A thought should be spared for the detachment of Grimsby police who had to cycle to Lincoln due to the lack of trains and arrived, exhausted, at 1am just as the riot was in full swing!

At this point Mr A D Bates was driving along Silver Street when he came across Inspector Milner, injured by the mob but protected by a 'giant' named Nimrod Ash. Bates took Milner in his car to find a magistrate and, at Deloraine Court, they got Dr Mansel Sympson out of bed. On the drive back to the centre of the city, Milner crouched over Sympson to protect him from missiles and staves while Bates drove like a demon. He later described the journey himself:

'Never before or since has any motor vehicle careered through the Stonebow and down the High Street at such a "hell for leather" speed and under official orders. Beer bottles, stones and bricks were thrown at us from both sides of High Street, but our speed saved us . . . Dr Sympson stood up in the car and read the Riot Act, the military fixed bayonets and raced up High Street at the double . . . those rioters scattered and ran.'

This account differs from that of the *Lincolnshire Chronicle*, which reported that the soldiers marched down the High Street with fixed bayonets at 2am but without the blessing of the Riot Act.

There were problems in other parts of the county too. At Grantham there was an attack on the South signalbox on the same night as the worst Lincoln disturbances. Victims of the strike included Skegness hoteliers and holidaymakers at Mablethorpe, who were 'marooned'.

On the morning of Sunday 20th August a notice from the Home Secretary was put up at the Stonebow, declaring that the railway strike had been settled. In the afternoon there was a march to the South Common, where the men decided to petition the Home Secretary about the provocative behaviour of the police.

Although the railway strike had been settled, there was still much bad feeling in the air. In Grantham four 'scavengers' employed by the refuse contractor were sacked and replaced by non-union men, while the dispute at Marshalls' Britannia works in Gainsborough threatened to turn ugly when pickets were 'bound over'. At the end of August the Bishop of Lincoln criticised the 'scanty wages' that many men received.

It seemed that the summer of discontent was over, but there was still scandal and recrimination to come. In November 1911 Mr Justice Ridley visited Lincoln as the Assize judge and pointedly snubbed the Mayor of the city by refusing to ride in his carriage or to talk to him. In reply, the Mayor refused to attend the Assize service at the cathedral. Ridley had pronounced feelings on the cause of the Lincoln riots, having noted that most of those involved were in the

On guard outside St Mark's railway station – extra police and soldiers had to be called in when the situation in the city threatened to get out of control. (Lincoln Local Studies Collection)

16 to 20 age range. He blamed the City Corporation for having failed to educate its young people properly, saying their behaviour was 'a disgrace to the town and the authorities'. In fact only nine people received short prison sentences as a result of the riots, which had shocked the city and hit the national headlines.

Lincolnshire Goes
to War

★

Throughout much of 1938 and early 1939 newspaper head-lines were concentrating on the gathering international crisis caused by Adolf Hitler's aggressive policies. Many experts predicted that the coming war would be one that air weapons would dominate. Accordingly, the Government began all sorts of schemes to prepare its armed forces and its civilian population for what was likely to happen. Lincolnshire's position as a frontline county was brought into focus by a huge air defence exercise that was organised for early August 1939.

The exercise involved a mass attack on Lincolnshire by the bombers of 'Eastland', which passed in waves over the coast at Mablethorpe and headed inland to bomb 'Westland'. Although Westland fighters were sent out to repel the attackers, the Eastland bombers got through to their targets. Lincoln and Gainsborough were both 'bombed' while the opposing forces fought dog-fights over Louth and Digby. Luckily all this was an exercise, for it was clear that defences were unable to protect Lincolnshire's centres of population – a serious situation given that many expected enemy attacks to include poison gas once the real war began. The only real casualty was an 'Eastland' bomber that suffered engine failure over Reepham and crash-landed in a field – managing to squeeze beneath some power cables that ran across the land there.

The air exercise was also used to test the preparedness of the civil defence schemes. Lincoln itself was 'blacked out' for most of the night, though as normal life was also expected to continue some lights were left on at major traffic bottlenecks like the High Street and the Stonebow. A number of other ARP exercises were also conducted.

On the last Sunday in August a special Peace Service was held at Lincoln Cathedral, but preparations for war went on regardless. At dawn at 1st September 1939, Hitler's forces began pouring into Poland – setting into motion the events that were to bring Britain into war two days later. At the very moment that Hitler's dive-bombers were attacking Polish troops, special evacuation services were being run in England that brought Lincoln its first real activity of the war.

The villages around Lincoln had been selected as a safe area to bring evacuated children to and on 1st September eleven trains were run from Leeds to Lincoln to bring children from the endangered Yorkshire metropolis. The first trains left Leeds at 8.30am and they continued to run throughout the morning, but observers at Lincoln Central station reported that they were arriving barely half full; 4,249 children were expected, but only about 2,000 arrived on the first day of evacuation.

The children got off the train in something of a daze, many of them never having been out of Leeds before. One child arrived with a bucket and spade, his parents having believed that all Lincolnshire was just like Skegness. The children were given two days' food supplies and taken to special billeting centres in schools around the city, such as St Giles and Skellingthorpe Road. From there, they were taken to their actual billets – some of these were in Lincoln itself, but most were in North Kesteven or the Welton area.

The ARP services spent 1st September in hectic activity throughout the county. White lines were painted on roads to help traffic during the blackout and trenches were dug in numerous places. In Lincoln both commons were dug up for trenches and an exhibition of church plate at the Usher Gallery was closed down. The needs of the Women's Land Army were widely advertised and by 1st September the Lindsey branch had acquired 171 recruits; apparently most of these were from Grimsby. Within the next fortnight this had risen to 344, by which time ten women were actually 'in

Digging an air raid shelter in Peel Street, Lincoln in September 1939, just one of the precautions taken in the county as war became reality. (Lincolnshire Echo)

place'. One of these was Lincolnshire's first woman tractor driver, Mrs Flossie Drummond at Middle Rasen.

Britain entered the war on 3rd September, forcing local authorities to make many momentous decisions. East Kesteven Rural District Council held an emergency meeting at Sleaford that day and resolved to buy a radio – so that it could listen to government instructions. The Chief Constable issued guidelines and instructions about the blackout, placing especial emphasis on care about bedroom windows and skylights. People were warned that nightly patrols would watch for offenders. Some local schools closed down when the first news of war came through, but others re-opened quickly, especially ones with air raid shelters like Skellingthorpe Road in Lincoln.

Evacuation from Leeds continued apace, but not without some confusion as 1,200 children were sent to Caistor – all in the apparent belief that they would be living in the town.

Since this would have virtually doubled Caistor's population, it is just as well that they were actually distributed to surrounding villages like Snitterby.

Lincoln City FC finished off with a win over Gateshead and its players then dispersed. Some joined the ARP service while others got local jobs. The team still came together for occasional friendlies – there was a game later in September against Nottingham Forest. The Lincoln team included a Horncastle man who was actually a Carlisle player and a Northampton player who had got a wartime job in Lincoln.

During the first real week of war public transport was cut back severely. This made it impossible for many pupils at de Aston School, Market Rasen, to get to their lessons and home again, so the school had to increase its number of boarders. By this stage there were also 1,700 Leeds schoolchildren in Lincoln alone, all of whom needed some form of education. Roundhay School started to share the facilities of Lincoln School and some buildings in Bailgate, presumably the Assembly Rooms, while Leeds Girls' High School moved in with its Lincoln equivalent.

News of the first Lincoln casualty of the war also came through on about 15th September. He was Stoker Lound of the Royal Navy and left a widow with five children. Due to wartime censorship, no details of his death were given.

Lincoln's first wartime 'scandal' occurred on 18th September. At about 8.30pm 34 lights on Burton's large shop in the High Street came on, lighting it up like a Christmas tree. No-one could be found to switch them off and a large and hostile crowd gathered outside the shop, suspecting a Nazi plot to bring the bombers to Lincoln. In fact a time switch had developed a fault, but the shop manager was not at home. He was eventually contacted by flashing up a message during cinema performances. A few days later the manager was fined 40s.

A number of other blackout offences came to court in the first weeks of the war, but they were mostly to do with motoring. A series of cases at Gainsborough all ended with £1 fines.

Large places like Lincoln and Grimsby had seen considerable ARP activity by mid-September, but the smaller villages were feeling neglected. The villagers at Colsterworth had been told by a government ARP official that small villages did not need air raid warnings – Colsterworth did not even have a telephone to connect them to the official system. The poeple of Barkston were also incensed at their isolation.

The fears of Colsterworth and Barkston proved to be groundless at this stage of the war. The 'phoney war' had begun and by the end of September people were beginning to relax. A lot of the Leeds evacuees returned to their parents so that plans for a Market Rasen evacuees' centre were abandoned – only five mothers and children were left in the town.

For Lincolnshire war became a matter for the factories of Grantham, Scunthorpe and Lincoln and later for the bomber pilots of the local airfields. Lincoln itself did not experience any casualties from air raids until March 1941.

Rock and Roll
at Bardney

★

Most fashions arrive a little late in Lincolnshire, and the 1968 'summer of love' with hippy fashion, drugs and 'free love' did not begin to affect local people until 1971. It arrived in the shape of the Bardney Folk Festival and was followed in 1972 by a massive rock and blues jamboree over four days. For a while the name of Bardney became as hallowed on the lips of a British hippy as the name of Woodstock was on his American counterpart's – much to the distress of some of Bardney's people.

Bardney, a large village on the banks of the Witham and looking downstream over the expanding vastness of the fens, was not a place that was used to the headlines. Over the centuries the people of Bardney had enjoyed a fairly placid existence, rarely troubled by the vagaries of fashion in the outside world. So the local people must have been rather worried when they heard that a folk festival was to be staged at Tupholme in July 1971. It was organised by Fred Bannister Productions with the help of William Hardy, a Tetford farmer who owned the Tupholme estate which included the Manor and the old ruined Priory. The site was chosen, according to Wendy Bannister, as it was the 'prettiest' available; she said that 'for a concert like this you must have a beautiful setting.' Such high-sounding words did not ease fears of drug-crazed hippies wandering the lanes of Bardney!

News of the planned festival was not greeted with universal enthusiasm. Some local people were reported to have a 'nasty feeling' about the imminent arrival of 15,000 hippies, while the local council would only rent out its waste disposal vehicle at an inflated rate. However, artistes booked included a number of major names of the time including The Byrds and James Taylor.

The folk festival was planned to be a one-day event but people began to arrive several days before. There were 'vast hordes of young people, long-haired and multi-coloured' according to one reporter, while on the Friday night Lincoln itself took on an unusual appearance. The High Street 'from one end to the other was full of young pilgrims laden with sleeping bags and rucksacks and the cathedral and art gallery grounds looked more like refugee camps than tourist attractions.'

Other commercial interests prepared for the big day in their own ways. A bakery delivered 4,000 large loaves, 800 sliced loaves and 30,000 ham rolls, but an old Bardney shopkeeper was reported as having laid in stocks for the rush by ordering an extra dozen loaves – hopefully she made it a baker's dozen.

The day itself was a great success, with some estimating the crowd at up to 60,000. Despite the huge numbers, the event was peaceful. Superintendent Carey said that, 'There's been no trouble at all . . . we have been very pleased indeed.' There was a slight problem when the ring fence was breached by some who wanted free music as well as free love, but the gap was plugged by burly security men hired from the Lindum Rugby Club. Wooden toilets were pulled down and used for firewood and a farmer complained of the theft of a tractor battery.

The event attracted international attention with TV crews from Japan, Mexico and Spain. Film actress Britt Ekland enjoyed the day and James Taylor was so struck with Tupholme that he wanted to spend another six months 'hanging out' at the Manor. Even the weather was good and although one or two complained of noise, most Bardney people found that their worst fears had not been realised.

The success of the 1971 festival attracted the attention of a promotional company called Great Western, whose control-ling interests included the actor Stanley Baker and Lord

Harlech, the former ambassador to Washington. Great Western selected Bardney as the site for a proposed four-day rock and blues festival that was to take place in May 1972. After contacting Bill Hardy, it was announced that the Tupholme site was to be used again and a bill of international stars was put together; this included famous names of the time, such as the Beach Boys and Joe Cocker, but also showed a canny knack of selecting those who were to become more famous later – Rod Stewart, Roxy Music and Genesis.

Some felt that the Great Western festival, offering a different type of music, would bring a totally unacceptable crowd to Bardney. A letter appeared in the press saying that 'rock and blues' would attract 'Hell's Angels and other undesirable groups, hell-bent on causing trouble . . .' Fears were exacerbated by reports of the scenes at the infamous Weeley festival in Essex.

A local chemist began to organise opposition to the festival, and this was encouraged by some wild press speculation – reports claiming that up to 200,000 were likely to attend the event though only about 45,000 actually turned up! To counter this threat, Baker and Lord Harlech flew into Bardney by helicopter and gave the Vicar a £10,000 'bond' as a deposit against any damage. Stanley Baker also held a 'meet the people' session in the village hall, which was packed with about 500 curious locals.

Baker blamed 'inflammatory statements made by people from outside the village' for causing so much fear and trepidation. He emphasised that Great Western were expecting no more than 50,000 music fans at the site and that proper services would be laid on. A suggestion that Lord Harlech's lands in Wales be used instead was turned down – they were too remote and rugged. However, some local people supported the festival and a pop fan collected a 700 signature petition in favour of it.

The opposition of some of the Bardney residents attracted all sorts of attention. Yorkshire TV dubbed the village 'Squaresville '72', which prompted a retort that the

American 'hippy' era had culminated in the Sharon Tate murders.

Opposition to the festival was also mounted by local councils, including the Horncastle RDC and Lindsey County Council although some councillors such as Spooner and Bramley supported it. The councils hoped to use the courts to ban the festival altogether, but were rather surprised when Horncastle's own health inspector wrote to the court to say that he was satisfied with the toilet arrangements and thought there was no danger of infection; the press promptly reported that he had been 'suspended for giving evidence in the case'.

The court hearings were a protracted affair with a farmer complaining of the nuisance caused by the 1971 festival. A Horncastle Council official said that, 'Any suggestion that the site is ideal for the festival is in my opinion misconceived.' The legal battle ended in a draw – the judge ruled that the festival could go ahead but that any nuisance committed would result in its promoters being guilty of a contempt of court.

As the festival approached local traders got prepared. Mr Constable of the Angel Hotel ordered an extra 6,000 pints of beer – four times his normal supply. Preparations were hit by a storm only a few days before things were due to start, with the stage and many marquees being damaged. To balance this was a success with the Hell's Angels: when a group of them arrived from Manchester to act as 'hot dog security men', they were persuaded to leave after receipt of their travelling expenses.

As the fans began to arrive, local and national newspapers sent reporters to Bardney to watch the scene and question local people. 'On Tuesday the fans were streaming into the village and the old folk just gazed at the young pop seekers with quiet animosity,' one report declared. A local butcher said that 'the pop fans seem to be very well-mannered and some talk very well.' A Mr R Conboy complained that he couldn't get a drink at his local as it was too crowded.

One of the village grocers took on an extra four staff and

Lincolnshire papers reported the Bardney Festival in detail. Despite widespread opposition to the event, it was a peaceful affair, marred by the terrible weather conditions.

there was much favourable comment that the Bardney shops were charging their normal prices. A butcher commented that 'I suppose it's only the same as living in a seaside resort during the summer.' The publicans did especially well – The Black Horse sold over 1,200 gallons of beer, The Nag's Head increased its normal sales tenfold, and The Jolly Sailor sold over 200 times its normal quantity of brown ale; the latter was probably due to the appearance of the group Lindisfarne at the festival, who had championed the merits of Newcastle Brown.

Perhaps one of the surprise 'hits' of the festival was the Bishop of Lincoln, Kenneth Riches. He had felt that the 1971 event was a success, and voiced his support for another festival during the days of the legal battle. He sent a letter to the press explaining his views: 'My concern is that the Church and all people of goodwill should try and understand why such large numbers of young people gather together for these occasions . . . I believe that many of them are seeking a meaning in life which they have not found in our materialistic society.' The Bishop spent Saturday night at the festival and held a service on Sunday morning.

The show was stolen though, not by one of the acts, but by the weather. Having given the site a good battering before the music began, foul weather returned on the Friday with low temperatures and unstoppable rain. It became so bad that about 700 people had to be treated for exposure, while local people rallied round by opening up the church and the hall as shelters. One paper referred to the whole site as a 'muddy marsh'.

Despite the weather, the festival passed off well. The *Daily Express* declared it 'victory for the Fans' since their good behaviour ensured that Baker and Harlech did not have to go to prison. However, the event ran about £25,000 over budget due to the cost of repairing the storm damage.

The police were much more active at the 1972 festival than at its predecessor. About 700 officers were involved, though many of these were on traffic duty, with the operation costing an estimated £100,000. It was reported that 124 arrests were made, including 82 for drugs offences. The CID set up a base at Langleys Farm but had few serious cases to deal with. Most involved the drugs squad, such as a man fined £150 for delivering a package of cannabis, LSD and dexadrine.

One of the few events to hit the headlines sounded lurid and sordid indeed. 'Man Danced Nude on Tables' screamed the banner headline in the *Echo*, reporting on an event at The Angel. In fact the man came from just down the road in Wragby and the amount of damage caused was overestimated by a factor of ten!

After all the fears, Bardney escaped without gangs of Hell's Angels marauding through the streets or drug-crazed hippies going on the rampage. The Parish Council chairman concluded that, 'We seem to have got off lightly . . . I have met some very well-behaved young people.' He was probably pleased, though, that rumours of a 1973 festival starring the Rolling Stones came to nothing.

Two Days of
Disaster

★

Lincolnshire has been known for many years as a county
with strong RAF connections. During the Second World War
the airfields were buzzing with tales of heroism and tragedy,
but after the war many of the airfields closed down and can
now only be recognised by old hangars in use as farm buildings or strips of concrete between the fields. Flying did
continue from some bases, and tragedy continued as well. In
January 1953 the county was struck by air disaster on two
consecutive days.

January 5th, 1953, was a foggy night in much of Lincolnshire. At Claxby Pluckacre, near Revesby, Miss Mary Ashton
was thinking about going to bed while her father, Albert,
was already tucked up under the blankets. At nearby
Miningsby Grange, 16 year old Tom Pennington was outside
getting coal. Suddenly they were all disturbed by the
thundering roar of aero engines overhead. 'That aircraft is
flying low!' Mary exclaimed, as it made every loose thing in
the house rattle with its vibrations. Tom was struck by the
'spluttering' of the engines. Then there was a tearing thud;
'Oh my God, it has crashed,' Mary shrieked.

Mary dashed from the house into the fog, but even in the
terrible conditions she could see the blazing wreck 300 yards
away across the fields. She dashed across the rough ground
through the fog, and was soon joined by other villagers from
the nearby cottages. Albert Ashton leapt from his bed and
came to join them.

The people clustered around the blazing wreck of the
RAF Washington bomber, which had been returning to
Coningsby. Five of its crew struggled out more or less

112

unharmed through a top hatch in the fuselage. With the help of the villagers they used axes to hack at the wreck and threw earth onto the flames so that they could drag an injured man from the blaze. They managed to pull him out through the top of the wreck although he had been pinioned across the legs by an engine, but five other men perished in the crash. Some of the crew were so distraught and shocked that they had to be restrained from running off into the night.

Inquiries afterwards show that the pilot had become confused in the foggy conditions as he approached Coningsby after a flight of over four hours. Flying too low because of the fog, the Washington bomber had struck a tree, crashed to the ground and burst into flames. Although fire crews attended from Horncastle, Spilsby, Skegness and RAF Coningsby itself, there was little they could do to save those who died. The injured man was taken to the RAF hospital at Nocton, where his condition improved slowly.

Just as the county was reading the reports of this disaster, another occurred — and one that was even more mysterious in its causes. Initial reports spoke of a Harvard training aircraft having come down with considerable force in a field about 300 yards from Hall Farm at Cranwell. It hit the ground with such an impact that the engine was completely buried and the rest of the plane 'piled over it'. At first there was no understanding as to what had happened — it had passed over Hall Farm with its engines running normally and the crew were familiar with the area. It was snowing at the time, and the first search party sent out had great difficulty finding the wreck.

On 20th January an inquest was held into the Cranwell crash. Although a verdict of misadventure was recorded, this covered considerable confusion as to what had happened. Corporal Cutler, a radio mechanic, had heard the engine clearly, saying that it 'revved up, then down, then up again.' He looked up and saw the plane come through the clouds, which were at 300 ft, in a vertical dive straight into the ground.

Richard Mitchell had been working in the fields 400 yards south of Cranwell village. He heard 'a big report, like a clap of thunder or a gun going off.' It was Mitchell who discovered the wreck and the two bodies.

The controller said that the plane had asked to be talked down through the low cloud and had descended to 500 ft, when it had unaccountably climbed back to 2,500 ft before beginning its precipitous and fatal final dive. The final story will never be known.

Zeppelin!

★

During the 19th century the proud British nation had been able to boast that the strength of its Royal Navy made it secure against attack from foreign forces, such as those led by the detested Napoleon. For 900 years, it was boasted, England had been a match for overseas adventurers who were kept at bay by the waters of the Channel and the North Sea.

Against this background of seeming inviolability, the early months of the Great War must have caused agonies of self-doubt in the hearts of the British people. In the opening stages of the war, the Germans scored a morale-boosting point by launching a naval attack on British coastal towns such as Scarborough and Hartlepool. As if this was not a sufficient blow to the pride of the Royal Navy, the Germans had also developed a weapon that made Britain's naval defences virtually useless – the Zeppelin.

The first airships to be used in war to any significant extent were those built by the French during the Franco-Prussian war of 1870, but those were largely built to carry messages. By 1914, however, the German engineers under the control of Graf von Zeppelin had designed airships that were capable of making a return journey to England and of dropping significant quantities of bombs. As if overnight, the Englishman's boast that he could sleep soundly in his bed had been destroyed, and the sea alone was no longer enough to give Britain a sense of security. The shock and horror which greeted German bombing of civilians in their own homes was reflected in local newspaper reports as Lincolnshire found itself in the front line.

One of the most determined Zeppelin attacks on Lincolnshire occurred on 31st January 1916, when Scunthorpe was raided. At 10.45pm the sound of Zeppelin engines was heard and L13 spent some time over the town, dropping explosives and incendiaries. A bomb was dropped at the upper end of Ravendale Street, damaging four houses. The Zeppelin then passed over the glebe pit, dropping incendiaries, and a bomb caused damage in Trafford Street. It turned back towards the Trent works and dropped a bomb which fell through into the sewer at the Waitlands. Many people panicked and 'fled' from the town into the neighbouring countryside, some even in their night-clothes.' Others were braver – when an incendiary landed in 86 year old Mrs Markham's house, she drenched it with a bucket of water and got a neighbour to throw it out of the window. The Scunthorpe attack continued with two bombs near the North Lincoln works and a bomb killing two men at the Redbourn Hill iron works. The Zeppelin passed over the chemical works and failed to drop anything on the Frodingham steel works where the blast furnaces were blazing away, but a bomb fell on a railway siding near the station. Bombs dropped on the old Lindsey works wounded Superintendent Holmes in the leg and a bomb that landed near Dawes Lane claimed the third fatality, Mr Benson.

At 6am on 2nd February 1916 the captain of the Grimsby trawler *King Stephen* found the wrecked Zeppelin L19 in the North Sea. Sixteen Germans were clinging to the wreckage, but Captain Martin decided not to rescue them since they would outnumber his own crew of eight. He decided to look for a patrol ship but could not find one, so he reported the wreck when he got back to port the next day. By the time help arrived, all the Germans had drowned. Two months later, on 23rd April, the *King Stephen* was sunk by a torpedo boat and its crew imprisoned in Germany. It was rumoured that this was a carefully planned revenge attack.

A major target for the Germans was the port and industrial complex around Immingham and Killingholme, but it was also one of the best defended parts of the county with guns and an airfield. On the night of the 5th March 1916, L11 dropped four bombs on Killingholme and the same night

L11's attempt to bomb Grimsby was thwarted by low cloud.
The most serious incident to affect Lincolnshire occurred
on 31st March 1916. The L22 dropped 26 bombs on
Humberstone, damaging a farmhouse. It then went on to
Cleethorpes, where one of six bombs dropped scored a
direct hit on a chapel in Alexandra Road where a number of
soldiers were sleeping. Thirty one men were killed and had
to be buried in a communal grave, while 53 were injured.
The council offices in Cambridge Street were also damaged
and another bomb landed in Sea View Street. On this crucial
night the naval air station at Cranwell was out of action due
to a breakdown in the telephones.

Most of the raids were far less effective. On the night of
28th July 1916, L13 crossed the coast at North Somercoates
and dropped two bombs near Fiskerton to no great effect
except to provide extra work for local glaziers; it dropped
further bombs on the villages south-east of Newark. The

*Two postcards showing Zeppelins over Scunthorpe. These may be faked
pictures produced for a local market stunned by the horror of the new war
from the skies. (Scunthorpe Museum)*

same night L24 unloaded its deadly cargo over Immingham, Killingholme and East Halton – the casualties amounting to one cow.

Lincoln was a prime target for Zeppelin attacks because of its engineering works. The city authorities did their best to impose a blackout. In 1916 James Smith was out late at night in the High Street and, having had a few drinks, decided to light a cigarette; he was arrested for striking a match 'in such a manner that it might serve as a land mark, guide or signal to enemy aircraft.' He was fined £1.

On Saturday 23rd September 1916 a number of Zeppelins raided London and Manchester. Late that evening one of the Zeppelins, L14, approached Lincoln but was shot at by the gun on Canwick Hill. It turned away from the city, and dropped a number of bombs either side of the river Witham near Washingborough. Four bombs fell within a space of 50 yards near the village, smashing windows in its main street and uprooting a pear tree.

The Baptist chapel at Cleethorpes was destroyed by a bomb dropped from a Zeppelin in March 1916. Thirty one soldiers who had been sleeping there were killed and 53 injured.

Other bombs fell either side of the river, breaking windows in a cottage beside the Lincoln to Greetwell road. The driver of a train on the Lincoln to Grimsby line had seen the Zeppelin overhead, and stopped in a cutting near Greetwell for shelter. This gave rise to a popular story that the Zeppelin had been following the train, hoping it would lead the way to Lincoln, which was blacked-out. When the train stopped, the Germans had assumed it was in Lincoln – and so unloaded their bombs, killing a couple of rabbits and three birds! A report in the *Echo* in 1957 alleged that the Zeppelin pilot had worked in the foundries in Lincoln and so knew all about the area.

The following day crowds of people left Lincoln to view the damage left by the Zeppelin and to collect souvenirs. Many of them wanted to use the old ferry across the Witham at Washingborough, which belonged to the local parish council. Normally it was operated by the passenger pulling it across the river with a chain, but on Sundays it was in the charge of 69 year old George Moore. He could not cope with the crowds brought along by the war damage.

People crowded onto the ferry and there was some 'larking about'. The ferry was rather overloaded and Moore found it impossible to pull it away from the side of the riverbank as its bottom had grounded on a shallow shelf there. When it began to list to one side, there was a surge of people across to the other – and the ferry capsized. Of the 25 people on board, two drowned when they were trapped underneath it and several others were lucky to survive. The two dead were both from Lincoln – Ernest Robinson (aged 17) of Carlton Street and George Nelson (7) of Winnowsby Lane. Fred Cooke had been collecting souvenirs and was pulled underwater by the weight of bomb fragments in his pockets; he became unconscious and was discovered only when Percy Allen stepped in the shallow water and trod on his face. Two local solicitors, E M Burton and T Maynard Page, received praise for helping to rescue the survivors.

The survivors were taken to the nearby railway station at Washingborough where the stationmaster gave out

Some bombs fell on open countryside, leaving craters such as this one found in July 1916. (Lincolnshire Library Service)

blankets, and a special train took them back to Lincoln. The two dead were the city's only 'home front' casualties of the war.

There were various other attempts to bomb strategic targets at Lincoln. In April 1957 an interesting claim was made by Mr H Ladlaw. He stated that a Zeppelin had bombed the railway sidings at Pyewipe Junction only one night after the King's train had been stabled there. He took it that the Zeppelin was acting on intelligence information.

On the same night as the Washingborough attack, the village of Scartho received 14 bombs without anyone being even injured. Mr J Grantham was so pleased about this escape that he had a special monument of a marble column surmounted with an urn put up in the churchyard. Further

*In September 1916 Scartho suffered an attack of 14 bombs but no one
was injured. This marble column was erected in the churchyard in
thanksgiving.*

south on the same night, L31 attempted to bomb Sleaford but was scared away by gunfire.

A similar story to the one about the train at Greetwell and a Zeppelin was told about an incident at Nocton. It was reported that a driver on a Great Eastern train between Sleaford and Lincoln realised that a Zeppelin was following the glow of his engine firebox in the hope that it would lead to the city. The driver stopped in Nocton station and the Zeppelin pilot, assuming this was Lincoln, dropped his bombs into the nearby fields. The same report goes on to claim that the Zeppelin was later shot down south-east of Lincoln by a Royal Flying Corps pilot from Waddington, but there is no evidence of a Zeppelin having come down in Lincolnshire. More definite is that at least one of the Lincolnshire pilots was killed in 1917, when Lt H Solomon's plane caught fire as he was taking off from Gainsborough to intercept an airship.

The Germans were erratic in where they thought they were and where they had bombed. On 31st March 1916 the Zeppelins were elated by the belief that they had bombed a battleship in the docks at Grimsby, while on 25th September 1916 L22 reported that it had bombed Lincoln, when in fact its bombs fell on Sheffield.

There were a total of eleven Zeppelin raids on Lincolnshire, most of them in 1916. After that the Germans began to lose too many airships – shot down by guns and by aircraft. There were air bases at Cranwell and Killingholme, and guns protecting Lincoln. One of the problems was that the Zeppelins scored few direct hits – one airship used radio bearings to bomb Boston, but its bombs landed 65 miles out to sea! The final raid was on 12th April 1918 when Lincoln was 'visited' again but without result, while other bombs fell among the seabirds in the Wash.

Index

Acknowledgements

★

I am especially grateful to the staff of the Lincoln Reference and Local Studies Libraries for their help in providing me with many different resources, and also to the staff of the Lincolnshire Archives. I am also grateful to local people who have helped me with their own memories and materials, among whom I must mention Barry Taylor of Bardney. The most difficult part of this book has been the collection of the pictures – it is very sad that much of Lincolnshire's photographic riches has been lost or is in danger.

Printed sources used for this book include the following:

Stamford Mercury
Lincolnshire Chronicle
Lincolnshire Echo
Grimsby Evening Telegraph
The Times
Lincoln City Library *Abell Collection*
D Crowen-Hodgson *Revelations of an Imp*
G Dow *Great Central* (1959)
H E Dudley *History & Antiquities of Scunthorpe* (1931)
C Ekberg *The Book of Cleethorpes*
W Foster & Co *The Tank – Its Birth & Development* (1920)
H Grieve *The Great Tide* (1959)
J Morris *The German Air Raids on Britain* (1925)
B Mummery *Immingham – Creation of a Port* (1987)
R Rimmel *Zeppelin* (1984)
Sir E D Swinton *Development of the Tank* (1924)
C Wilson and S Seaman *Scandal* (1986)